Walker Percy: Art and Ethics

Walker Percy:
Art and
Ethics

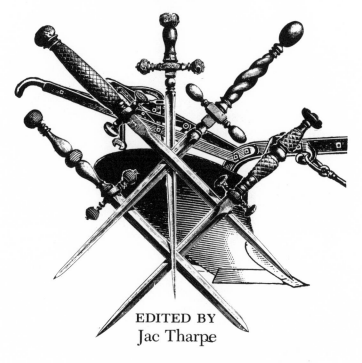

EDITED BY
Jac Tharpe

UNIVERSITY PRESS OF MISSISSIPPI • *Jackson*

for JOHN KANIA

Copyright © 1980 by
THE SOUTHERN QUARTERLY
Manufactured in the United States of America
Cover design by Larry Hirst

Library of Congress Cataloging in Publication Data

Main entry under title:

Walker Percy, art and ethics.

  Bibliography: p.
  1. Percy, Walker, 1916-   --Criticism and
interpretation--Addresses, essays, lectures.
I. Tharpe, Jac.
PS3566.E6912Z95   813'.54   80-12227
ISBN 0-87805-119-8
ISBN 0-87805-120-1 (pbk.)

Contents

Preface

Preparations for this collection began more than two years ago when both *The Message in the Bottle* and *Lancelot* were very much on the minds of students of Walker Percy's work. *Message in the Bottle* seemed to offer an unlimited number of topics worth study, and *Lancelot* appeared to be so distinctly a new way for Percy that everyone had an interpretation. But while these essays concentrate on these two works, the collection gradually expanded in size and in range. Besides the several interpretations of Percy's last novel and examinations of aspects of *Message in the Bottle*, a complete bibliography and a brief review of criticism are contributed to further study of Percy's work.

John Edward Hardy examines the opening scenes of each novel for its statement about place. His observations are especially revealing in the discussion of *Love in the Ruins*, wherein so many places are symbolic, the cusp of the interstate, Paradise Estates, and, at the end, Tom More's garden and finally his bed. Lancelot begins his narrative with an invitation specifically "into my cell." He is associated with various other enclosures—the pigeonnier, the corncrib, his house. His proposed utopia in Virginia is yet another place. The subtitle of the essay suggests that the beginnings of the novels are related to the endings of the characters.

Lewis Lawson, who continues his series of essays in explication of Percy's existentialist sources, shows how the particular movies Binx sees explain and exemplify important concepts in Percy's thinking. Lawson's observations enrich ideas such as repetition and rotation that have nearly become submerged in the superficial everydayness of Percy criticism.

Charles Bigger explains Percy's use of *queer* in the subtitle to *The Message in the Bottle* by examining some aspects of Heidegger's *Introduction to Metaphysics*. Heidegger's own translation of the famous chorus from *Antigone* about man's situation in the universe emphasizes the unique strangeness of man's being—his queerness.

These notes for a longer study of Percy's anthropology give fascinating insights into the background from which Percy views the act of naming that distinguishes man from all other creatures.

Michael Pearson's opening comments about Percy's theory of language are designed to introduce his observations about the insufficiently studied theory of art, which Percy has discussed in a symposium held at Washington and Lee in 1975 (published in *Shenandoah*) as well as in *The Message in the Bottle*. These ideas lead to an attempt to show how *Lancelot* differs from the earlier works while also elaborating a theme important to Percy's study of modern culture. *Lancelot* at times purposely reflects the misuse of language that Percy deplores.

Jay Telotte is also concerned with Percy's theory of art, but he first attempts to show the significance that C. S. Peirce has for Percy's concept of man's fate. This concept of symbolization, of knowing, is involved, as *Message in the Bottle* is intended to show, with communication and with man's failure to be "uniquely human." Intersubjectivity, Telotte says, is heightened through the narrative process.

Robert Brinkmeyer, Jr. uses "Notes for a Novel about the End of the World" and "The Message in the Bottle" as implicit statements of Percy's novelistic intent. With this theoretical apparatus, he attempts to show how Percy speaks to those who know their despair and deliberately jolts the complacently unaware. *Lancelot*, on which he concentrates, is designed, he thinks, to force readers to reject Lancelot and choose Percival. The priest represents the old via dolorosa and not the rosy way of the scientific humanists.

Susan Kissel feels that *Lancelot* is a distinctly Roman Catholic novel with a message that humanism, even love, is rejected as Christians again take up the sword, "the only means these Christian heroes have of restoring life to a lost and blinded world," she says. To arrive at this conclusion, she examines important parallels with Flannery O'Connor, as other students have done, and she adds a comparative study of the Roman Catholic writer J. F. Powers.

Corinne Dale uses Malory and Dante to resolve the ambiguity of *Lancelot* and discern a clear message in Percy's contrast of Percival and Lancelot. Her study of Lance's purgatorial journey shows how parallels with *The Divine Comedy* hint at the only possible artistic resolution of the action and intent.

Jerome Christensen concentrates on the enigmatic signs visible from Lance's cell window and discusses the meaning of the other messages Lancelot receives—such as the I-O of Siobhan's blood type. *Ma* symbolizes the large, important theme whether women are ladies or whores and what the men are who make and label them. The feminine is also Columbia, America, and the original pristine Virginia, land of the virgin. Christensen uses this fragmentary sign for a fascinating interpretation of the whole novel.

The unusual essay of Cecil Eubanks is neither linguistic, aesthetic nor literary in its subject matter. The author's thesis is that while Percy is much concerned with intersubjective communication and comprehension of the fundamental good news of the Christian message, he appears to dismiss concerted political reform or activity of any kind. Eubanks says that for Percy "politics is an abstraction, fundamentally incompatible with the searchings of a sovereign wayfarer." That is, can the sovereign wayfarer participate in the attempt to improve the world in which he is cast away?

One of the main features of this volume is the comprehensive bibliography, complete to about January 1, 1980. For the first time, some of the snarls in the primary bibliography are untangled.

Finally, Randolph Bates briefly discusses the three books that have studied Percy's work, concentrating on Panthea Broughton's recent collection of essays, and mentions a few of the many articles listed in the bibliography.

All quotations in this volume are from the Noonday paperback editions of Percy's works, published by Farrar, Straus and Giroux, except that the hardcover edition of *Lancelot* is used. Abbreviations of titles are obvious. Double quotation marks are avoided even when dialogue is quoted. For the convenience of the reader, in some cases main points have been italicized.

J.T.

Honors College

Walker Percy: Art and Ethics

Since everyone is saying "Come!" now in the fashion of apostles—Communists and Jehovah's Witnesses as well as advertisers—the uniqueness of the original "Come!" from across the seas is apt to be overlooked. The apostolic character of Christianity is unique among religions . . . But what if a man receives the commission to bring news across the seas to the castaway and does so in perfect sobriety and with good faith and perseverance to the point of martyrdom? And what if the news the newsbearer bears is the very news the castaway had been waiting for, news of where he came from and who he is and what he must do, and what if the newsbearer brought with him the means by which the castaway may do what he must do? Well then, the castaway will, by the grace of God, believe him.

(last paragraph of "The Message in the Bottle")

Percy and Place:
*Some Beginnings and Endings**

JOHN EDWARD HARDY

> This morning I got a note from my aunt asking me to come for lunch.
> I know what this means. Since I go there every Sunday for dinner
> and today is Wednesday, it can mean only one thing: she wants to
> have one of her serious talks. It will be extremely grave, either a
> piece of bad news about her stepdaughter Kate or else a serious talk
> about me, about the future and what I ought to do. It is enough to
> scare the wits out of anyone, yet I confess I do not find the prospect
> altogether unpleasant. (*M*, p. 3)

From this remarkable first paragraph of Walker Percy's first published
novel we learn, or we can infer, a good deal about the character and
mentality of the first-person narrator. Perhaps, if we are shrewd and
experienced enough as readers of novels, we can predict something of
how the plot will develop.

But the whole thing, for all its easy, colloquial tone, is curiously
detached. The voice is vaguely twentieth-century American. That is
about all one can say. The narrator, the unnamed aunt and her step-
daughter Kate, might as well be living in New York or San Francisco as
in New Orleans. The present "action"—he has received the note in
the morning, but we do not know precisely how long he has taken to
start thinking about it—is entirely cerebral. Absolutely no physical
setting is indicated, not even so much as to tell us whether the speaker
chooses to do his thinking indoors or outdoors.

It is not until we get to the second and third paragraphs of his
narrative, in which he treats us to certain reminiscences, first of his
childhood, and then of the very recent past, that Binx (or Jack, as he is
first called) begins the process of orientation and that we discover him
to be, indeed, quite extraordinarily sensitive to his environment.

*This paper was read, in slightly different form, at the Downeast Southern Renas-
cence Conference, University of Southern Maine, Portland, 30 October 1978.

Consider his recollection of the street behind the hospital, where, when he was eight years old, his aunt took him for a walk to tell him that his older brother had died of pneumonia.

> It was an interesting street. On one side were the power plant and blowers and incinerator of the hospital, all humming and blowing out a hot meaty smell. On the other side was a row of Negro houses. Children and old folks and dogs sat on the porches watching us. . . . We walked slowly in step. "Jack," she said, squeezing me tight and smiling at the Negro shacks, "you and I have always been good buddies, haven't we?" "Yes ma'am." My heart gave a big pump and the back of my neck prickled like a dog's. "I've got bad news for you, son." She squeezed me tighter than ever. "Scotty is dead. Now it's all up to you. It's going to be difficult for you but I know you're going to act like a soldier." (pp. 3–4)

Putting together certain features of the aunt's idiom and bearing and of Binx's description of the scene—notably, the phrase "Negro *shacks*" (italics mine) which he uses in referring the second time to the row of houses—we can now fairly definitely locate the action in a Southern city. Further, of course, the details of the setting which Binx so vividly recalls, the particular sights and sounds and smells, tell us things about his personality and psychic history, about the nature of his sensibility, that could not be quite so clearly revealed in any other way. And, finally, we understand that the aspects of cultural history reflected in the scene, its "Southern" features, are in the overall design of the novel probably more than accidentally related to Binx's personal concerns.

In the third and fourth paragraphs, when Binx recalls going to a movie the month before in a suburb "out by Lake Pontchartrain," the identity of the city in which he lives—presumably the same one in which his brother Scott died—is established, perhaps the more effectively for the fact that its name is still withheld. Again, the scene is recreated in exact and vivid detail. The nearly empty suburban theater is described as a "pink stucco cube, sitting out in a field all by itself. A strong wind whipped the waves against the seawall; even inside you could hear the racket" (p. 4). After the movie—about an amnesiac who "found himself a stranger in a strange city . . . [and] had to make a fresh start, find a new place to live, a new job, a new girl" (p. 4)—Binx and his own then current girlfriend stand outside the theater talking to the manager, and now it is the sounds of the movie that intrude upon the drama of nature. "It was a fine night and I felt very good. Overhead was the blackest sky I ever saw; a black wind pushed the lake toward us. The waves jumped over the seawall and spattered the street. The manager had to yell to be heard while from the sidewalk speaker directly over his head came the twittering conversation of the amnesiac and the librarian" (p. 5).

In the minds of most readers, identification of the city as New Orleans can be expected almost immediately to awaken certain exotic fictive associations, against which Percy ironically plays off what at first glance might seem to be the rather pokey everydayness of his suburban-moviegoing hero's adventures. One of the novel's central themes, that of the relationship of art and reality, thus subtly introduced in the non-naming of the fabled city, is then developed in the description of the immediate physical setting.

Binx's recollection of the scene begins, of course, the extended history of his career as moviegoer. And the attentive reader will very soon discover the relevance of the amnesiac's story to Binx's own "real-life" situation, and the reasons why the previously recorded childhood reminiscences should in turn have reminded him of his attendance at this particular movie.

Such is Binx the moviegoer's peculiar disposition—"but perhaps," to quote another of Percy's novels, "nowadays it is not so unusual" (LG, p.3)—that his most affectionate "home thoughts" should not only always remind him of his estrangement, but remind him of it in a way that is distinctly pleasurable. We cannot explore here all the subtleties of the question whether Percy is or is not a "novelist of alienation," or of what he meant when he said that "There is no such thing, strictly speaking, as a literature of alienation" (MB, p. 83). But one of the ways in which he is different from many others who write about alienated characters, anyway, is that in his novels we always know very distinctly what the character is alienated from: I mean, simply, the forms of the social tradition from which he is separated. Further, it is remarkable in this novel that, although we might detect in what I have called the curiously detached quality of the opening paragraph a hint of the speaker's alienation, when we come to the first passage actually describing an experience of alienation the final effect is somehow to make us feel right at home. Binx might be somewhat eccentric in his choice of places to enjoy. But the place is beautifully realized for us, and he communicates his joy in it. Moreover, the art of the realization is of the most solidly traditional novelistic sort.

At the beginning of *The Moviegoer*, the hero-narrator simply begins speaking, directly revealing what he is thinking and feeling about the note from his aunt, without bothering to tell us where he is. The opening scene of *The Last Gentleman*, the only one of Percy's four novels narrated in the third person, also presents a young man in the act of thinking. But the emphasis is exactly reversed.

"One fine day in early summer a young man lay thinking in Central Park." The narrator tells us *where* the young man is doing his thinking, indicates the general quality of the day and specifies the season, but does not bother to tell us *what* he is thinking, or even what he is thinking about.

The one sentence is the whole of the first paragraph. The second continues: "His head was propped on his jacket, which had been folded twice so that the lining was outermost, and wedged into a seam of rock. The rock jutted out of the ground in a section of the park known as the Great Meadow. Beside him and canted up at mortar angle squatted a telescope of an unusual design" (p. 3).

The narrator seems bent on getting everything firmly in place—the jacket, folded just so, in the seam of the rock, head of thinking young man on the jacket, mortar-angled telescope planted on the ground beside him; the part of the park in which rock, man, and telescope are located precisely identified—before proceeding with his story.

In fact, even then he does not satisfy our curiosity immediately. Instead, he jumps ahead a moment, to indicate that something of radical importance is *about* to happen to the young man. Then he pauses, for two paragraphs of generalized description of the hero's personality and his psychological problems, and another on the ambiance of day and park, before picking up the thread of present action. And still the emphasis is more on place than on any of the other elements of human action that might be stressed: motive and intent, passion or reason, a sequence of cause and effect. It appears belatedly in passing that the subject of the thinker's thoughts is simply the peculiar quality of the park itself, the environment of his thinking:

As for the park, green leaves or not, it belonged to the animal kingdom rather than the vegetable. It had a zoo smell. Last summer's grass was as coarse and yellow as lion's hair and worn bare in spots, exposing the tough old hide of the earth. The tree trunks were polished. Bits of hair clung to the bark as if a large animal had been rubbing against them. Nevertheless, *thought he* [italics mine], it is a good thing to see a park put to good hard use by millions of people, used and handled in its every square inch like a bear garden. (p. 4)

So much for our first question, about what the young man, physically situated as indicated in the first sentence of the novel, might be up to mentally. He is up to his situation, no more and no less. And when we come at length to the first, definite physical action, when the young man bestirs himself to squint into his telescope, we discover that the situation has not essentially changed. With the aid of the telescope, he has somewhat extended and severely narrowed his range of vision—the instrument is focused on a section of the cornice of a building, "no doubt one of the hotels along Central Park South" (p. 4), though one is unsure which, for "It was as if the telescope created its own world in the brilliant theater of its lenses" (p. 5)—but his basic orientation in the "real" world of the park is not disturbed.

At last, the narrator reveals what the young man's purpose was in coming to the park with the telescope. "He was waiting for the peregrine" (p. 5). And certainly it is a startling and gratifyingly original purpose. How pleased we are to learn that he is this singular sort of bird-watcher, instead of either the professional photographer, say, or the ordinary voyeur we might have suspected him of being. But the point I want to stress at the moment is that the whole interest of the falcon here depends upon the vivid sense of place that Percy has established in the preceding paragraphs. No doubt, the sight of such a bird even in the wilderness, especially with the aid of the young man's superlative telescope, would be thrilling enough. But the supreme excitement of his discovery here is the fact of its being totally unpredictable. The young man has seen the bird the day before, we are told, and hopes that it will come again, so that he can photograph it. But we know, without being told, that at least one of his reasons for wanting to photograph it is that he could "hardly believe his eyes" the first time. The great wonder of the falcon is its being so *out of place* in the urban

setting. The significance of the traditional name of the species—
peregrine, the alien, the wandering falcon, the pilgrim—in its relevance to the young man's character and fate, has been thoroughly
explicated by Martin Luschei in *The Sovereign Wayfarer*.[1] Upon the
young man whose besetting problem is, the narrator has told us, that
he "had to know everything before he could do anything" (p. 4), and
who yet, we are soon to learn, is himself the wanderer in a strange
land, the alien, who on most occasions is unlikely to be assured of
anything before he is required to act, the apparition of the falcon
understandably exercises a peculiar fascination. But the young man
himself does not, of course, experience the bird as a name, but as a
physical presence. To the extent that the passage describing the falcon
may be interpreted as a play on the name, the word *peregrine*, the
effect is the more brilliant for its being entirely dramatic.

Of course, as Luschei has noted, the young man turns out after all to
be, in a sense, the voyeur we might first have taken him for. The falcon
does not reappear. The momentous occurrence anticipated by the
narrator, the "chance event" which is to change the whole course of
the young man's life, is a case of mere girl-watching—"unusual,"
perhaps, to use one of the narrator's favorite words in these opening
pages, with respect both to the girls themselves and their poetic
note-passing and to the manner of the watching—but still nothing to
raise an experienced Central Parker's eyebrow more than an eighth of
an inch, inevitably, I am afraid, something of an anticlimax to the
exercise in falconry. But, again, and also "of course," the girls are
necessary to advance the plot; we could hardly be so avid of novelty as
to require that Percy have the young man fall in love with the hawk.
And, however disappointing it may be in other respects, the principal
effect of place-consciousness is not diminished in this episode.

Our hero the pseudo-engineer and complete modern Southerner
—Percy allows the narrator a number of pages in the first chapter for a
kind of anecdotal essay on what it means to be a modern Southerner—has first of all to get his bearings, before he can pursue even his
natural curiosity, let alone his natural passions. When the falcon does
not reappear, he starts to dismantle the camera-fitted telescope, but
takes one last look through the lateral eyepiece as the barrel drops to
the horizontal:

> There in the telescope sat a woman, on a park bench, a white woman dark as a gypsy. She held a tabloid. Over her shoulder he read: " . . . parley fails."
>
> But when he looked up he couldn't find her. The telescope was pointed toward the southeast, where a thicket of maples bordered the Great Meadow. She could only be there. Yes, now he saw: the telescope looked toward a leafy notch and through it to the summit of one of the little alps which overlook the Pond. (p. 5)

And so on. He sees the woman conceal a note in a crevice at the back of the bench and then disappear, packs up his gear, surveys the terrain once more in naked-eye perspective, finds his way to the bench, takes the note out of its hiding place, reads it and replaces it, returns to his former post, sets up the telescope again, this time without the camera, waits for the intended recipient of the note to appear, and when she does—young, distinctly female, beautiful even, but somehow boyish, somehow startlingly resembling the young man *himself* (Percy is not embarrassed to employ a dash and exclamation point here)— immediately falls in love with her: "at first sight and at a distance of two thousand feet" (p. 7).

The chances are he would have taken no more than casual notice of the note-dropping if he had observed it from a neighboring park-bench, would not have thought of waiting for the second girl to appear. The telescoping, the two thousand feet of aesthetic distancing, are absolutely essential to his falling in love. Which is much the same thing as to say that there could have been no story, without the elaborate attention to setting with which Percy delays the start of his hero's adventures.

But, to return a moment to the question of the marked contrast between the opening paragraphs of *The Moviegoer* and *The Last Gentleman*, the crucial irony is that Will Barrett exercises his acute sense of place—what is, at least in part, an aspect of his Southern-ism—in a setting that defies cultural definition as a place. It is not simply that he, like the falcon, is "out of place." (And it should be noted, incidentally, that the falcon, so long as the supply of fat and slow-moving pigeons holds out, is not impaired in his essential func-tions by his urban exile.) In Central Park, everybody is out of place. Millions of people go there, tryst there, exchange notes there, resort there to rape and be raped, rob and be robbed, to eat their lunches and to pray and to beg and to despair, to feed the pigeons and pelicans, to murder and create. But nobody lives there. There are definable communities within New York City. But Central Park, of course, is not a part of any of them. It has no customs and no code of manners, not even any distinctive fashions. On one hand, the names of its topographical features might as well be the names of places on the moon. On the other, traversed by untellable thousands every day, it is the whole old, worn, weary, used earth itself, "and wears man's smudge and shares man's smell,"[2] this "zoo," this "bear garden." Either way, no place at all.

Not only its narrative method, but the fact that its hero is the only one who is physically displaced, both at the beginning and at the end of the action, distinguishes *The Last Gentleman* from Percy's other novels. If the other three heroes unquestionably have their own, perhaps inescapable desert places, still they have them, in the geographic as well as other senses, nearer home.

As we take leave of Will Barrett, he has just announced his firm purpose to go back, more or less "home," to Alabama. But if the project depends solely upon the counsel and guidance of the likes of Sutter Vaught, it promises still to be a long rough trip. Much more reassuring, it seems to me, than the prospect of his getting any further useful advice out of the good doctor is just the fact which we have already observed at the outset—that Will's traditional Southern sense of place appears to be readily portable. Fugues or no, if you can get your bearings in Central Park, you can get them anywhere.

> Now in these dread latter days of the old violent beloved U.S.A. and of the Christ-forgetting Christ-haunted death-dealing Western world I came to myself in a grove of young pines and the question came to me: has it happened at last?
>
> Two more hours should tell the story. One way or the other. Either I am right and a catastrophe will occur, or it won't and I'm crazy. In either case the outlook is not so good.
>
> Here I sit, in any case, against a young pine, broken out in hives and waiting for the end of the world. Safe here for the moment though, flanks protected by a rise of ground on the left and an approach ramp on the right. The carbine lies across my lap.
>
> Just below the cloverleaf, in the ruined motel, the three girls are waiting for me. (*LR*, p. 3)

With his first two novels, it would appear that Percy at least temporarily exhausted his interest in the young man as hero. Even in *The*

Last Gentleman, Sutter Vaught threatens at times to become more interesting in his own right than as reluctant mentor to Will Barrett. In *Love in the Ruins*, the aging, derelict physician is both unrivalled protagonist and his own narrator.

Besides the subtitle "The Adventures of a Bad Catholic at a Time Near the End of the World," the intricate calendar-scheme of the narrative—which begins on the Fourth of July in an unspecified year, executes some dizzying flashbacks on that ground, jumps back to July 1, then works forward day by day once more to the Fourth, and finally leaps ahead in a short concluding chapter somewhat in the nature of an Epilogue to a Christmas Eve five years later—is likely to direct the reader's primary attention to considerations of time rather than place. Just how near the end of the world is it, we might like to know, that these holidays are celebrated? Or, to put the question another way, just how long after "our own time"—roughly the time, that is, of the novel's composition and publication?

The internal evidence is confusing. Except for the Bantu uprising, there is not much on the socioeconomic and political scene that could not have been anticipated in the late sixties. In certain aspects of technological development, the times seem much advanced: for example, Toyota has developed an understandably popular automobile with only one moving part. On the other hand, it appears that Gore Vidal, improbably elevated to the status of "grand old man of American letters" (p. 19), is still alive and writing. There are, to be sure, generalized references to great advances in gerontology as well as automotive design. Perhaps the implication is that Vidal has been kept alive, in body as in reputation, considerably beyond what he might have expected ten years ago. But one simply cannot be sure.

It will not take us long to tell that the confusion is deliberate. The novel is obviously not standard futurist sci-fi, the product of a naively inverted historicist mentality. Neither is it a piece of earnestly muddled doom-saying. Unquestionably, one must try finally to come to terms with it as a story of spiritual quest. But, first of all, it is a satiric fable. Inverted historicism and muddled doom-saying are among the more obvious targets of the satire. It is a fable, simply, of the "modern" Western world, more specifically of the modern U.S.A., whose time is notoriously neither then nor now, a time notoriously "neither wrong

nor right."[3] Further, with reference to the purposes both of the satire
and of the quest story, it is worth noting again that the principal action
occurs at holiday seasons: in a "time out of time," a time not of history
but of myth.

There are similar uncertainties in the fictive geography. Again deliberately, I think, Percy has made it difficult for us to identify the
locale as any particular part of a particular state with which we are
historically familiar. We are left free for some time to keep wondering
just where in the old dispensation we are: in Louisiana, Mississippi,
Alabama or Georgia, perhaps Florida? All things considered—
references to the More family history, swamps, pirogues and Cajun
paddling style—probably South Louisiana, if by this time all things
are considered, and if anyone is still interested in such homely matters.

But we must stay interested. Luschei has done a good job in analysis
of the "geography" of the novel—sometimes he calls it "landscape" or
"terrain"—in its allegorical aspect. The town on the one side, Honey
Island Swamp on the other, and Paradise Estates between, plus Fedville to which otherwise irresolvable conflicts can be referred, are
terms in the flawed dialectic of contemporary culture. That the "geography" is vaguely "Southern" Luschei takes for granted; but Percy's
"vision encompasses the whole of the New Eden, the United States of
America" (p. 193).

And so it does. There is another aspect of Percy's art, however,
which escapes the dialectic altogether. And that is what I take to be
the novelist's central business: creating an illusion of the reality of
human experience, creating a character who impresses us as a real
man in all the complex immediacy of his knowing and doing, a real
man, blood, bone, muscle, brain and hair, doing something particular
in a particular time and place.

A particular place. It is instructive, once again, to take a closer look
at the opening pages. Of course, what this novel is rather centrally
"about" is disorientation: a fact hinted at in the very wording of the so
meticulously non-informative "stage directions" to the first chapter.
"In a pine grove on the southwest cusp of the interstate cloverleaf. 5
p.m./ July 4." What interstate? What states does it connect? What is its
number, and the number of the interchange, where in the southwest

cusp the pine grove stands? But there are no answers. That is the point. It is *the* interstate, the ultimate interstate. It does not connect any states. Interstates never did, really. The whole system was conceived as one long bypass. What's in a number? If you've seen one interstate, you've seen them all. And the same goes for all the other man-made structures the narrator sees from his station in the grove: the motel and deserted shopping center and drive-in movie, even the abandoned church, with its "barn and silo" architecture. Wherever ruins are left to mark the place of a vanished human community, it is a sight to inspire melancholy. But the most depressing thing about our contemplation of these ruins is the realization that they never did shelter activities definitive of anything that could properly be called a community. It is questionable whether the civilization that could produce such structures as these, in their total anonymity of design, their utter stylelessness and irrelevance to the surrounding countryside, was not already in ruins when the buildings went up and the concrete was poured for the parking lots.

"Now in these dread latter days. . . ." We know the time of day, and the day of the month, but that information is of little use to us so long as the year is not specified. Is there some vague astrological significance in the stage directions: "the southwest *cusp* of the interstate cloverleaf?" What manner of danger is it precisely that the narrator faces? He speaks of "waiting for the end of the world." The *interstate*, then, connects states of *being*. And yet he has taken his stand in the grove armed with a carbine! In view of all the uncertainty about what is going on, and when, it is not inappropriate that we should also be kept in the dark about where we are.

In due time, we are to learn the more or less rational explanation for the narrator's odd behavior. There are two—distinct, although possibly related—threats against which he must take measures to defend himself and his girlfriends in the motel. 1) There is a sniper after him; hence the carbine. 2) He has good scientific reasons to fear "within the next two hours an unprecedented fallout of noxious particles" in the area. "The effects of the evil particles," he explains, "are psychic rather than physical. They do not burn the skin and rot the marrow; rather do they inflame and worsen the secret ills of the spirit and rive the very self from itself. If a man is already prone to anger, he'll go mad

with rage. If he lives affrighted, he will quake with terror. If he's
already abstracted from himself, he'll be sundered from himself and
roam the world like Ishmael" (p. 5). Against the catastrophe of the
fallout—which might at least be interpreted not unreasonably as a
prelude to the "end of the world," if not actually equated with that
event—he assures us that he has armed himself with another and
highly secret weapon, of a design known only to him. Conveniently
pocket-sized, More's Qualitative Quantitative Ontological Lapsometer is an instrument with which he can not only evaluate the spiritual
condition of potential victims of the fallout, but inoculate persons
against its effects or, failing that, "cure them should it overtake them."

And, if all this might be otherwise only the more disquieting for the
sober and sensible reader, we ought already to have taken some
comfort in the opening description of the natural setting. There is
much else at work here somewhat to the same effect. The easy col-
loquialism and jocularity of the speaker's tone, for one thing. "Here I
sit . . . broken out in hives and waiting for the end of the world." If we
are not quite sure yet whether the whole eschatological bit is some
kind of joke, still the mention of the skin ailment eases tensions.
Prophet or plain nut as he may be, here in any event is a good-
humored, down-to-earth sort of fellow whom we feel we can go along
with for the moment. We recognize also the sympathetic parody of
literary and movie conventions in the scene—the gentle take-off on
the Western and the story of guerrilla warfare—as well as Percy's
allusions to episodes in his own earlier works: the wounded Binx
Bolling coming to consciousness in the Korean woods (see the prob-
able etymology of "carbine" in this connection), Will Barrett's exercises in Central Park with his telescope set at "mortar angle" to focus
on the hawk's perch atop the hotel. But in other and more fundamental
senses, too, we are after all on familiar ground here.

After the chilling solemnity of the opening phrases, there is something wonderfully reassuring about the speaker's description of his
situation in the pine grove. Here is the old, dear, dependable, fallen
world of our most primitive human experience. Images of mortality
abound. But if there is death in the earth, death in the air, it is death on
terms we understand, death as natural process, in which man shares
with the rest of creation. The man has the hives. The young pine tree

against which he sits has a tumor. But the disease of the tree admirably suits it to the comfort of the diseased man. With the growth on its trunk, it is "bowed to fit [his] back" (p. 4). The highway interchange, although useless now in the purpose of its original design, to move a heavy volume of automotive traffic on and off the freeway, offers advantages not only to the man in getting the drop on the sniper, but to the hawk that balances on a column of air rising from the heated surface of the cloverleaf's "concrete geometry." Our drunken hero Dr. More, surely no saint and at best a diffident Faustus, desperate hunter and hunted, finds himself for a moment charmed in a wistful harmony with his natural environment. The bird of prey hanging overhead, so ominous at first glance, is at last a figure of mortal beauty, executing as evening approaches its long glide across and down the sky to the refuge of the swamp. How comfortingly unpretentious the doctor is, "versed in country things,"[4] in his matter-of-fact observation on the flight characteristics of the species: "From the angle of its wings one can tell it is a marsh hawk" (p. 4). A bit later, a pair of circling buzzards replace the hawk in the sky over the interchange, for all that they maintain a much greater height affecting the watcher's morbid imagination still more directly. Yet, even with them he converses in a tone that is curiously joshing, a mood of grimly confident good humor: "Do I imagine it," he thinks, "or does one cock his head and eye me for meat? Don't count on it, old fellow!" (p. 6).

We know this place. We are in the deepest of senses "familiar" with it. But the familiarity depends, not upon any quality of the merely commonplace or typical in it, but rather, for all its complex allusiveness, upon the rich, sensual and emotional particularity of detail. If the scene is "universal" in its significance, it is so as the particulars partake of the archetype, not as they fit the scheme of an intellectual construct, the idealized landscape of allegory. In this quality of its "peculiar familiarity," as it might be called, the quality of seeming familiar at the same time that it is nameless, the opening scene of the novel powerfully foreshadows the Epilogue.

> Hoeing collards in my kitchen garden.
> A fine December day. It is cold but the winter sun pours into the walled garden and fills it up.
> After hoeing a row: sit in the sunny corner, stretch out my legs and look at

my boots. A splendid pair of new boots of soft oiled leather, good for hunting and fishing and walking to town. . . .

A poor man sets store by good boots. Ellen and I are poor. We live with our children in the old Quarters. Constructed of slave brick worn porous and rounded at the corners like sponges, the apartments are surprisingly warm in winter, cool in summer. . . .

Through the open doorway I can see Ellen standing at the stove in a swatch of sunlight. . . .

. . . A kingfisher goes ringing down the bayou. . . .

The bricks are growing warm at my back. In the corner of the wall a garden spider pumps its web back and forth like a child on a swing. (pp. 381–82)

The contrast is obvious: I do not mean to suggest any the less important for being obvious. At the beginning, the protagonist sits alone on a hillside, fugitive, homeless, childless, in imminent mortal danger and unshriven, a middle-aged alcoholic whose situation is only the more pathetic for his having not one but three women looking to him for love and protection. At the end, he is at home in his modest but charming apartment in the old slave Quarters, raising his collards and running his trotlines on the bayou before taking the bus to work, manifestly blessed in the poverty that has taught him the joy of simple possessions like a good pair of boots, in having now "only one wife to his name," to cook his grits and bear his children and keep him off the bottle, in the services of a priest who is willing to grant him absolution on the basis of an imperfect contrition but who insists as well on the obligation of penance. Even the images of death in the garden scene—the kingfisher, and the spider on its web—are unmistakably benign. But what the pine grove at the highway interchange and the collard patch beside the bayou have in common is that neither belongs to the schematized world of the town, Paradise Estates, Honey Island Swamp, and Fedville.

If Tom More is at last happily resolved to "cultivate his garden," it is essential to note that Percy's attitude toward that project is at least as complex as Voltaire's. For the aging and weary hero there is a danger here of succumbing to a romantic counter-faith which is, from Percy's orthodox Catholic viewpoint, potentially as deadly as the false humanism of Paradise Estates he has so luckily escaped. (The satire in this chapter on the return of the Ivorybilled Woodpecker as a kind of

Second Coming sufficiently defines the peril.) Thus, we must rejoice to observe that before the very end the doctor has patently sinned again. If not exactly lusted after his neighbor Mrs. Prouty, yet lusted after *her* lusting. Has very definitely got drunk again, drunk as a lord, for the first time in five years, and using Christmas as an excuse, worse yet. Worst of all, is still harboring hopes of perfecting his Lapsometer, the more shamefully for disclaiming to himself such "worldly" motives as the desire to win the Nobel Prize.

But all this serves only to emphasize again the quality of place that distinguishes the Quarters, *like* the pine grove, from the not-place of Paradise Estates. For all its undeniable and seductive charm, the marriage of primitive "tradition" to the primitive beauty of nature, life in the Quarters is unmistakably life in the fallen world. No one of the slightest intellectual sophistication, in the twentieth century or after, could possibly persuade himself that this is the best of all possible worlds. And that, precisely, is what makes it a *better* world, even from the orthodox point-of-view, than the world of Paradise Estates.

The implication is clear, I think, that the advantage for Dr. More of his final estate here is simply that it leaves him susceptible of grace. It is not itself the fullness of grace, not the place to be "prepared" according to the promise of his Savior. But the great virtue of his living there is that it does not deny him conviction of the necessity of grace.

When Dr. More totes his heavy and middle-aged "Presbyterian armful" of an Ellen off to her new $600 Sears-Roebuck bed at the end—"to bed we go for a long winter's nap . . . not under a bush or in a car or on the floor or any such humbug as marked the past peculiar years of Christendom, but at home in bed where all good folk belong" (p. 403)—the scene is hardly a solemn prefiguring of the celestial marriage. But neither is it simple parody. Rather—with infinitely wry apologies to *Clement* Moore, in addition now to the sainted Thomas and other ancient worthies—it sums up the purpose of the whole final chapter, to offer secular analogy to the divine truth. A sense of propriety, specifically the propriety of place, is not equivalent to active virtue. A man may dishonor himself and his wife in bed as well as on the kitchen floor, honor himself and her on the floor or under a bush or in a car. But, given a choice of place, the bed is—as they used to say

before humbug prevailed in the language of the moral theologians—
conducive to virtue.

In *Lancelot*, a novel that comes full circle in a number of ways—
might have been subtitled "The Movie*makers*"—Percy is back again
in New Orleans and environs. Of course, he tells us in the headnote
that the setting is not really New Orleans and the River Road, that city
and road are "place names of an imaginary terrain." But that is true of
cities and roads in any work of fiction. The tinkering with local geography that he goes on to catalog in the note—adjustments and substitu-
tions necessary, presumably, to suit the stage to the peculiar temper of
his hero's mind—involves no very radical dislocations. For my money,
the New Orleans that survives here is if anything more like the real
place than what, say, Tennessee Williams leaves us, not to speak of the
Superdome builders.

Again, the protagonist is his own narrator, speaking all but uninter-
ruptedly, both of past events and of his present situation, until very
near the end. The movements, gestures and facial expressions of a
single listener, the man named Percival, his occasional questions and
comments, are indicated in the narrator's responses. But only on the
last two pages does the monologue give way to anything resembling
dialogue, when in a series of italicized monosyllables (twelve *Yes*es
and one *No*, to be exact) Percival audibly responds to Lancelot's
questions. The words are still cryptic, at best. But they are enough at
least to reassure us, in case we had been tempted now and again
previously to question the narrator's reliability even on this point, that
Percival actually exists, and is physically present in the room.

That room, the setting of the novel's "frame narrative," the narrative
of the narrative, so to speak, will bear close examination. Lancelot
begins:

> Come into my cell. Make yourself at home. Take the chair; I'll sit on the
> cot. No? You prefer to stand by the window? I understand. You like my little
> view. Have you noticed that the narrower the view the more you can see?
> For the first time I understand how old ladies can sit on their porches for
> years.
> Don't I know you? You look very familiar. I've been feeling rather de-
> pressed and I don't remember things very well. I think I am here because of
> that or because I committed a crime. Perhaps both. Is this a prison or a
> hospital or a prison hospital? A Center for Aberrant Behavior? So that's it. I
> have behaved aberrantly. In short, I'm in the nuthouse. (p. 3)

He goes on to elaborate on the simple virtues of life in the cell. No matter whether the institution is properly to be classified as prison or hospital—having once sarcastically acknowledged the euphemism of the official name, he pointedly refuses to accept it—he assures his visitor that the cell itself "is not a bad place to spend a year, believe it or not." It is clean, dry, neither too hot nor too cold, has a high ceiling. The cot, chair, and desk are sufficient furniture for a man like him: one who is infinitely weary of life, and, the implication is, at the same time infinitely imaginative. And, besides, there is the view from the window. A single window, and narrow. But (one remembers Nick Carraway's words on the subject) Lancelot urges his visitor not to be too quick to assume he has taken in at a single glance all there is to be seen from there: "a patch of sky, a corner of Lafayette Cemetery, a slice of levee, and a short stretch of Annunciation Street" (pp. 3–4).

We may well suppose that something is to be made of the particular features of the scene mentioned—sky, cemetery, levee, street— besides, perhaps, the names of the cemetery and street. We can also anticipate that the narrator is soon to call attention to people he has seen moving about in the street and on the levee, and to offer his interpretation of the "found drama" of their actions. But, first of all, there is a half-obscured sign out there.

Instructing the visitor to "lean into the embrasure and crane to the left as far as possible," he tells him what he will see. There are three lines of lettering on the signboard, of which only the beginnings are visible. On the top line, an entire word—*Free*—can be made out, followed by an ampersand. On the next, indented to the right, a single syllable appears, *Ma*. At the bottom, still farther to the right, only the solitary capital letter *B* is discernible. He suggests a couple of intelligible wholes to which these fragments may belong. "What does the sign say? Free and Easy Mac's Bowling? Free and Accepted Masons' Bar? Do Masons have bars?" (p. 4). Although we do not know at this point, it is possible that the visitor is not, say, another patient-prisoner, but someone in a position to tell him what, in fact, the sign says, tell him, perhaps, whether Masons have bars. And it is notable that Lancelot does not wait for an answer to his questions.

In any event, what we have here is a "sign" that does not signify. And, at first glance, an observer who either does not really care what the sign says or positively prefers that its message remain a mystery. But, as it turns out, he does want to know what it says, but he does not want anyone else to tell him; he wants to find out for himself. Toward the end of the narrative, anticipating his release from confinement, he pictures himself leaving the building, strolling down Annunciation Street, turning the corner of Tchoupitoulas, and for the first time seeing the sign whole. "At last I shall know what it says" (p. 250).

There is a measure of whimsical self-mockery in Lancelot's portentous tone, of course. But he is serious enough, all the same. And in the whole opening scene, with its particular focus upon the unreadable sign at the street corner, there are important indications of the fanatical egomania which he is further to reveal in his tale of his past career as arsonist-murderer and his predictions of the role he will play in the future.

I have said that the opening paragraph of *The Moviegoer* is "curiously detached," in the sense that it provides absolutely no setting for the account of Binx Bolling's reflections upon the meaning of Aunt Emily's note inviting him to lunch. But if Kate is right in seeing Binx as an egotist—she calls him at one point "the most self-centered person alive"—and as habitually rather coldly abstracted in his pursuit of his "little researches," so that she must wonder what fate awaits her as his wife, it is fortunate that she never had the chance to fall in love with such a man as "Lance" Lamar. In the opening scene of *Lancelot*, there is detailed and insistent attention to the physical setting. And yet, it is a setting reduced to the bare essentials of physicality, the bare necessities of an enclosure suited to the occupancy of a creature possessed of a body as well as a mind. Lancelot refers to his cell as a "place," but it is such a place as hardly deserves the generic name of place.

The cell seems "not a bad place" to Lancelot for the simple reason that it offers nothing to distract him from his single-minded preoccupation with the high drama of his own existence, with the role he has conceived for himself as prophet and scourge in the last days of the world. And the "little view" from the window, so conveniently narrow, is to him merely an extension of the cell. It is not with any normal and healthy intellectual curiosity that he regards the changing scene outside, trying open-mindedly to make what he can of the phenomena that it falls to him to observe. His speculations about the "*Free & Ma*

B" sign, with the occult suggestions of the reference to Freemasonry, are something of a conscious joke. But he is, in fact, compelled to regard everything out there as a "sign." Not only the old women scrubbing tombstones in the cemetery on All Souls' Day, but bumper stickers on a battered Volkswagen, a girl who crosses the levee every day, the song she sings: all things must somehow "signify" in the scheme of his entirely private eschatology, even if he is not yet able to "read" them clearly.

The whole business of the "signs" probably has something to do with the issues of Percy's language studies: such matters as Susanne Langer's distinction between sign and symbol. But we cannot get into that here. Let it suffice to note the pseudo-scientific character of Lancelot's initial investigations concerning his wife's infidelity, his time-and-distance calculations on his own and Margot's movements during the period of Siobhan's conception, his inquiry into the genetic characteristics of blood types. The sign-mongering temper of his mind, although in a context that is at least superficially non-theological, is already apparent. He is not, of course, really the disinterested investigator here. He knows, at heart, what he wants to prove from the moment he begins his calculations.

Whatever else this novel may be about, it is about violation, about desecration and defilement. The violation of humanity, finally, of human bodies and human souls. But, somehow centrally, the violation of place. The place of human habitation: a house, first, then the earth itself.

Margot's "restoration" of the pigeonnier is itself a seriocomic instance of defilement, although the shoveling-out of the "150 years of pigeon shit" would appear superficially to indicate the contrary. Consigned there simply as adjunct to his wife's little "project," with time on his hands in more senses than one, and a brain not so far deteriorated as Margot might have counted on, Lancelot makes his first sinister discovery in an entirely appropriate setting. And, notwithstanding the fact, which he himself recognizes, that he has all along acquiesced in his victimization, our primary sympathies must be with him as the violated, not the violator.

It appears that the invasion of the godling moviemakers, with their artificial thunder and wind, evil magicians in whose craft the unholy marriage of all the worst in all the ages of the decline of dramatic art and the advancement of technology is daily celebrated, is only the latest in a series of breakings-and-enterings in which Margot has actively conspired with the intruders. It is hard to say just what is the last straw. Perhaps the discovery that the movie people have undertaken to corrupt Lucy. (Or pseudo-discovery, it should properly be called. Lancelot ostensibly wants sure evidence, proof, before he acts. But Elgin cannot deliver it. What he brings is only another collection of "signs" intelligible only with reference to the system of Lancelot's madness.) In any event, we cannot fail to sympathize with the abused man's sense of outrage: the righteous fury of his need at last to cleanse his house of the abomination.

The trouble is, of course, that he succeeds in cleansing it only by destroying it, a measure that must be regarded as extreme by any standards. Such an action might still be forgivable if undertaken in the heat of rage. But it is a cold fire with which this man destroys. He is a cold-blooded murderer if ever there was one. All manner of pride motivates him: personal pride, the pride of his insulted masculinity, social pride, intellectual pride that is somehow peculiarly in his case the *mask* of social pride. But it is at least as important to note the means he chooses as it is to define the motive of his crime.

With a kind of monstrously sardonic humor, and using Elgin in a way that is the ultimate modern refinement of racist exploitation, he outdoes the moviemakers at their own game of turning the house into a "set." While they in the innocence of their accustomed corruption go about making their movie, he is secretly making his. And very bad movies they both are; but his is the worse, and not alone in the technical sense that so embarrasses Elgin. He cynically "uses" the house itself, not only as instrument of murder, but as instrument of its own destruction.

The terror of the whole proceeding, especially of the final, close human encounters in the desecrated old house, the doomed couplings, is undeniable: there is little in modern literature to equal Percy's performance here. Pity for the human victims is another matter. But if we must be tempted to feel that the only pity of it is that the whole caboodle did not go up with the house—that the human beings deserve, if anything, worse than they get—the house, on the other hand, not Lancelot's house, but his ancestral house, deserves better.

There is no human justification that I can see for Lancelot's escaping the destruction of Belle Isle except to tell his story—a story that is inconceivable without the house, and that could not conceivably be told without the larger setting of the city which surrounds the prison-hospital. At the end of the novel, when the totally unrepentant, now universally vengeful madman, anticipating his release, announces to Percival his plans for a "new beginning" in the Virginia Blue Ridge, he does well to wonder whether the converted corn-crib Anna has offered him as a temporary refuge is not merely a new version of Margot's pigeonnier. All things considered, the outlook is not good, *especially* if Anna should, as he hopes, still decide to accept his offer of marriage, and if he should, as he intends to do, regain custody of Siobhan.

Of course, much may depend upon what it is that Percival wants to tell him at the end. (Lancelot asks: "Is there anything you wish to tell me before I leave?" Percival's *"Yes"* is the last word of the novel.) A good many critics seem to feel rather sure of themselves about what is on Percival's mind here, or at least about the general significance of his series of monosyllables. Perhaps *Walker* Percy—who is, by the way, as clearly distinguishable from his namesake in the novel as he is from Lancelot—really is sure. But from the complete text of the novel as we have it one thing seems to me very clear, that Lancelot's madness begins and ends in a fundamental disrespect for the reality of the world outside himself. The Virginia he envisages, as the place of his "new beginning," does not exist. And the chances are—barring some miraculous reform, cure, to be worked by Percival's further revelations—he will be exceedingly dangerous when he learns that the Commonwealth is unwilling to accommodate the rough beast of his imagining.

NOTES

[1]Martin Luschei, *The Sovereign Wayfarer* (Baton Rouge: Louisiana State Univ. Press, 1972).

[2]Gerard Manley Hopkins, "God's Grandeur."

[3]Robert Frost, "Acquainted With the Night."

[4]Robert Frost, "The Need of Being Versed in Country Things."

Moviegoing in
The Moviegoer

LEWIS A. LAWSON*

John Bickerson "Binx" Bolling, of New Orleans, the narrator of
Walker Percy's first published novel, certainly lives up to the epithet
which serves as title. During the eight days of the novel proper, he
refers to twelve specific and several unidentified movies and to
thirty-seven actors and eight actresses. During the same time, he goes
to the movies no less than four times, including a drive-in on Saturday
night. His appetite seems indiscriminate: he sees *Panic in the Streets*,
with Richard Widmark, on Wednesday night, an unidentified western
on Thursday night, *Fort Dobbs*, with Clint Walker, on Saturday night,
and *The Young Philadelphians*, with Paul Newman, on the following
Monday night. The reader soon accepts as true the confession that
Binx makes early in his narration: "The fact is I am quite happy in a
movie, even a bad movie" (*M*, p. 7).

It is not surprising that several commentators have spoken of the
role of the movies in the novel.[1] Despite considerable critical interest,
though, there has been no extended study of moviegoing as the central
theme. Such a study must begin with the realization that Binx has not
always been an avid moviegoer: "Until recent years, I read only
'fundamental' books, that is, key books on key subjects, such as *War
and Peace*, the novel of novels; *A Study of History*, the solution of the
problem of time; Schroedinger's *What is Life?*, Einstein's *The Universe as I See It*, and such. During those years I stood outside the
universe and sought to understand it. I lived in my room as an Anyone
living Anywhere and read fundamental books and only for diversion

*I wish to acknowledge the support of the General Research Board of the University
of Maryland during the writing of this essay.   L.A.L.

took walks around the neighborhood and saw an occasional movie. Certainly it did not matter to me where I was when I read such a book as *The Expanding Universe*. The greatest success of this enterprise, which I call my vertical search, came one night when I sat in a hotel room in Birmingham and read a book called *The Chemistry of Life*. When I finished it, it seemed to me that the main goals of my search were reached or were in principle reachable, whereupon I went out and saw a movie called *It Happened One Night* which was itself very good. A memorable night. The only difficulty was that though the universe had been disposed of, I myself was left over. There I lay in my hotel room with my search over yet still obliged to draw one breath and then the next. But now I have undertaken a different kind of search, a horizontal search. As a consequence, what takes place in my room is less important. What is important is what I shall find when I leave my room and wander in the neighborhood. Before, I wandered as a diversion. Now I wander seriously and sit and read as a diversion" (pp. 69–70).[2]

The vertical search fails Binx because of the methodology employed by such "fundamental" books as *The Expanding Universe* and *The Chemistry of Life*. Binx's experience of suffering alienation from his immediate world by virtue of his practice of the scientific method is very reminiscent of twentieth-century existential/phenomenological charges against the practitioners of objectivism. The methodology of scientific empiricism, using ever more elaborate, complicated technology for the gathering of data, enables its practitioners to make ever broader and more penetrating generalizations about the nature of things. But scientific methodology, often thought these days to be the primary, indeed the only, apprehension of reality, actually considers a thing "stripped of all instrumentality," as Jean-Paul Sartre, one of Percy's formative influences, puts it, in *Being and Nothingness*.[3] By "instrumentality" Sartre means that a human being considers a thing originally as it relates to him as a tool, an instrument, a utensil, and then only secondarily as it is a composition of properties and characteristics. Thus science tempts its practitioners to reverse modes of apprehension, indeed finally to forget the specific existence of the thing, all the more to concentrate upon its objective qualities. Then a thing would have, in Sartre's words, "purely external relations,"[4] so that it would appear in exteriority as distant and separate as a star in the sky.

But, in the consideration of a thing, if instrumentality is left out, then man is left over, for it is, after all, man to whom the thing as instrument has referred. No doubt this exclusion of man from a binding relationship with the things which he sees accounts for the widespread feeling that Western man seems more and more alienated from his world even as he develops the technology to quantify it with greater and greater precision. Binx, as a reader of "fundamental" books, learns to measure the immensities of space, but discovers himself to be "left over," as he says, or *"de trop,"*[5] "superfluous," as Sartre puts it.

Even though denied by the scientific-empirical technique and its hoard of data, Binx accepts his "exile" (p. 89). All that he can establish is that he is *not* the object that fascinates him, the world, so he lives in Sartre's state of "fascination": "In fascination there is nothing more than a gigantic object in a desert world. Yet the fascinated intuition is in no way a *fusion* with the object. In fact the condition necessary for the existence of fascination is that the object be raised in absolute relief on a background of emptiness; that is, I am precisely the immediate negation of the object and nothing but that."[6] Binx's search thus becomes "horizontal," as he begins to wander a *"desert world"* or "a world without men,"[7] a world of space, rather than place.

Obsessed by his fascination, which he calls "wonder," Binx moves to the middle class suburb of Gentilly, "a desert if there ever was one," says Percy in an interview.[8] Out there, "where the world is all sky" (p. 73), Binx has "lived ever since, solitary and in wonder, wondering day and night, never a moment without wonder" (p. 42). What he likes about Gentilly, where he lives in an apartment "as impersonal as a motel room" (p. 78), is that his street, Elysian Fields, "is very spacious and airy and seems truly to stretch out like a field under the sky" (p. 10).

Out there he organizes his life around emptiness. He seeks the "deserted playground" (p. 10) of a church across the street from his apartment for his evening ritual of studying the newspaper movie page for his night's outing. It does not matter to him, if the theater is nearly empty, though he does cultivate the acquaintance of theater employees, for their familiarity offers a boundary to his emptiness: "If I did not talk to the theater owner or the ticket seller, I should be lost, cut loose metaphysically speaking. I should be seeing one copy of a film which might be shown anywhere and at any time. There is a danger of slipping clean out of space and time" (p. 75). With that anchor of the known, he can range in the deserts of his fancy, as he does when he talks with the movie cashier about her son: "He is stationed in Arizona and he hates the desert. I am sorry to hear this because I would like it out there very much" (p. 74). Similarly, he can sit in his office, the sphere of the known, and read his one-book library (p. 78), *Arabia Deserta*; hiding the book inside a Standard and Poor binder, Binx offers a telling action, for he is the outwardly successful businessman who really conceives of himself as a ghost wandering a deserted space.[9] He stresses this identification when he reveals his response to *Fort Dobbs*, the movie that he sees at the drive-in, under the stars: "in the movie we are in the desert. There under the black sky rides Clint Walker alone. He is a solitary sort and a wanderer" (p. 143).

Percy does not make a random choice when he selects *It Happened One Night* as the movie for Binx to see just after he has disposed of the world by generalization, but finds himself left over in fact. The very title itself is significant: "it," the "it" of the "I"/"It" dichotomy, the overwhelming *en-soi*, did happen that night, when Binx concluded that the material world was all and that he was nothing. Beyond the suggestiveness of the title, however, is a reference to that particular movie in an essay which Percy had written just about the time that he was writing *The Moviegoer*. In "The Man on the Train: Three Existential Modes,"[10] Percy discusses the problem that contemporary alienated man has with time. Simply stated, Percy's thesis is as follows: contemporary man all too often feels that his life is inauthentic, is immersed in "everydayness." In "everydayness," a term borrowed from Martin Heidegger's majestic *Being and Time*, man falls into a "they-self" system, in which he accepts the standards of the public— the public media, the public institutions, the public worldview—in place of any reflective conception of himself. He listens to what "they say"; he does what "they do." He deliberately hides within the swarming mass of society by doing nothing to distinguish himself from the average, the typical, the ordinary, the acceptable. If he has a vague apprehension that his life is actually without meaning and substance, then he casts about for an alternative.

The only real alternative would of course be to confront the unsatisfactoriness of the present, to struggle for authenticity by an acknowledgement of one's alienation, but it seems to be much more common that the sufferer looks to either the future or the past for the meaning that will transform the present. If he turns to the future, he values the rotation, the orientation toward the radically different future that enables the sufferer to ignore the dreary present. If he turns to the past, he attempts to discover the point at which his life got off the track, in the hope that he could go back to resume his life at that point. This pondering of the past is called repetition. Both of these terms, *rotation* and *repetition*, are familiar in existential literature.

In "The Man on the Train" Percy uses *It Happened One Night* to illustrate rotation, which is alternately called "zone crossing." There is, to begin with, the subject/object split. If we accept the assertion that the subject is nothing but that which observes, then we are left with the subject entirely dependent upon the object, which only overwhelms and bores. What, though, if the subject could vary the object that he observes? Then he would have novelty, would not be bored, could perhaps convince himself that in some new surrounding he would discover the possibility of being something himself. It is vitally important for the alienated man, then, to be able to cross zones, escape from one environment in order to pursue possibility in another, "pass on impassible as a ghost" (*MB*, p. 88).

Zone crossing, then, is the kind of wandering that Binx decides to do, once he has discovered that the scientific method has excluded him from his world. He will of course view any new object as a part of the "gigantic object in a desert world"; incapable of any "fusion with the object," he will apprehend his world as he views a movie. In *Being and Having*, Gabriel Marcel, another of Percy's influences, establishes a very similar metaphor.[11] There are two modes of detachment: the one of the saint, the other of the spectator. The saint participates in the very core of reality by his indifference to the manifest appearance of the universe. The spectator is characterized by a curiosity, "a form of lust" about the " 'cinematographic' representation" imposed on the universe by the scientific technique, and thus "alienation" occurs. "I am not watching a show," Marcel promises to remind himself daily, but Binx Bolling deliberately chooses that behavior. In the novel, then, moviegoing characterizes the alienated man's fascinated gaze at a distant reality, stresses the sense of apartness that he feels.

Binx himself quite obviously understands moviegoing as a symbolic action that illustrates his relationship to the objective-empirical world. On occasion, as when he sees *Panic in the Streets*, he seeks the apparently reassuring—but ultimately deadly—confirmation of his own experience that a scientific formulation offers; this objective "proof" of subjective apprehension Binx calls "certification": "Nowadays when a person lives somewhere, in a neighborhood, the place is not certified for him. More than likely he will live there sadly and the emptiness which is inside him will expand until it evacuates the entire neighborhood. But if he sees a movie which shows his very neighborhood, it becomes possible for him to live, for a time at least, as a person who is Somewhere and not Anywhere" (p. 63).

Generally, though, Binx seeks movies that present patterns of rotational behavior that he might emulate, as for example *Fort Dobbs* or an unnamed movie that he has recently seen: "The movie was about a man who lost his memory in an accident and as a result lost everything: his family, his friends, his money. He found himself a stranger in a strange city. Here he had to make a fresh start, find a new place to live, a new job, a new girl" (p. 4). Such movies stimulate the fantasies that Binx concocts for himself and a girl observed on a bus: "If it were a movie, I would have only to wait. The bus would get lost or the city would be bombed and she and I would tend the wounded" (p. 13).

The devising of zone crossings is now Binx's basic effort in life; by night he goes to the movies and by day he lusts after his secretary, Sharon, sexual novelty being the highest rotation. If all else than himself is the "It," to which he cannot really be joined, then seduction, laying hands upon a part of that "It," would be a delightful pretense that he can in fact touch his world. When they go off for the weekend to the Gulf Coast, he so fascinates her that she wants only to be touched: "Sharon cleaves to me as if, in staying close, she might not see me" (p. 136), Binx tells us, as he leads Sharon to his mother's supposedly deserted fishing camp. But the family is (surprise!) there, and, rather than the seduction, taking his half-siblings to the movies occupies Binx that night. He shows no disappointment, though, for he has already achieved his intention, in making Sharon acknowledge her availability to be touched. In fact, since rotation concerns anticipation rather than participation, possibility rather than actuality, then her potential seduction is preferable to the *fait accompli*: Binx is ever on the threshold, but does not have to suffer the inevitable disappointment that accompanies the failure to maintain transcendence through the sexual act. Rather, Binx thinks that his being able to please his siblings, especially his afflicted brother Lonnie, and his seeing such an appropriate movie as *Fort Dobbs* are bonuses to an already enormously successful escape from his "everydayness." He sums up his exultation: "A good night: Lonnie happy . . . , this ghost of a theater, a warm Southern night, the Western Desert, and this fine big sweet piece, Sharon." Then he draws his conclusion: "A good rotation. A rotation I define as the experiencing of the new beyond the expectation of the experiencing of the new" (pp. 143–44).

Fort Dobbs must be a most rewarding experience for Binx, for it mirrors his image of himself, presents his life to him as a stylized performance, objectifies his subjectivity (which the subjectivity cannot do for itself, of course). Binx wants to live his life, in other words, as if it were a role in a Western movie. In "The Man on the Train" Percy draws an existential meaning from that classic American genre: "The I-It dichotomy is translated intact in the Western movie. Who is he, this Gary Cooper person who manages so well to betray nothing of himself whatsoever, who is he but I myself, the locus of pure possibility?" (*MB*, p. 94).

As a moviegoer, Binx is aware that he must employ the appropriate gestures, if he is to impersonate a person of unrealized possibilities, act like the stranger in a Western movie. He assumes the role expected of him on any occasion. Mostly he patterns his behavior after movie stars, those creatures of "resplendent reality" (p. 17), as he characterizes them: "Toward her I keep a Gregory Peckish sort of distance" (p. 68); "it comes back to me how the old Gable used to work at such jobs: he knew how to seem to work and how to seem to forget about women and still move in such a way as to please women: stand as sweat

with his hands in his back pockets" (p. 95); "It is possible to stand at
the window, loosen my collar and rub the back of my neck like Dana
Andrews" (p. 105). On an occasion when "everydayness" is van-
quished by the novelty of an automobile accident, Binx is able to act
like a romantic hero, and he exults: "O Tony. O Rory. You never had it
so good with direction. Not even you Bill Holden, my noble Will" (p.
127). For once, Binx feels free of the "malaise," which he defines as
"the pain of loss. The world is lost to you, the world and the people in
it, and there remains only you and the world and you no more able to
be in the world than Banquo's ghost" (p. 120).

Binx's nighttime disguises seem obvious enough, especially since
he frequently tells us whom he is impersonating. But he adopts a
daytime disguise that he does not acknowledge; this identity purports
to be genuine: "I am a model tenant and a model citizen and take
pleasure in doing all that is expected of me. My wallet is full of
identity cards, library cards, credit cards. . . . It is a pleasure to carry
out the duties of a citizen and to receive in return a receipt or a neat
styrene card with one's name on it certifying, so to speak, one's right to
exist. What satisfaction I take in appearing the first day to get my auto
tag and brake sticker! I subscribe to *Consumer Reports* and as a
consequence I own a first-class television set, an all but silent air
conditioner and a very long lasting deodorant. My armpits never stink.
I pay attention to all spot announcements on the radio about mental
health, the seven signs of cancer, and safe driving . . ." (pp. 6–7).

Such slavish adherence to the model behavior of the consumer.
Binx would have us believe that the advertising industry and the
communications media invented him! He is making himself into a
mechanical man: just as much as Sartre's waiter, he is playing at being
what he says he is. Describing a waiter who is elegantly excessive in
acting like a waiter, Sartre explains such posturing as the waiter's
expression, to the sufficiently perceptive, of his contempt for his own
role. There is more to him than just being a waiter; that *more* is his
consciousness. He is conscious of himself as a waiter, hence is supe-
rior to his actuality, transcends his factual nature.[12] Binx is, in other
words, engaged in a pattern of bad faith.[13]

Binx wants to live, then, as a consumer of new products and sensory
experiences, but never to chance an authentic emotion. The most that

he can tolerate is an occasional bout of the malaise, a weak nausea that signals a revulsion against a confining, threatening world.[14] Yet it is precisely through emotions, even nausea, that Binx could gain reentry to the world denied him by the objectifying media. For it must be an emotion that makes an "I" aware of his facticity, that is, the fact that he exists as an actuality.

Take the emotion of fear, which Heidegger uses as an example in *Being and Time*.[15] Binx acknowledges that in Korea, in combat, while lying wounded, he felt in touch with things and made a vow to search for a meaning for his life, if he lived (p. 10). *Being and Time* would explain his behavior thus: Fear is one of the avenues through which Dasein, the "I," comes to itself or finds itself.[16] Dasein becomes open to the disclosure that it dwells in an existence in whose creation it had no part, that it dwells within a confine that is both limiting and limited, and that what it confronts in that confine is of vital significance to it, so that it must be responsible for itself, despite its lack of control over its origin. Fear, then, is an outstanding example of one of the states-of-mind, that ontological characteristic by which Dasein is made aware of the actuality of its placement in the world.

In Korea, Binx had, by virtue of his fear, become aware of himself as a fact. But at the same time, he had vowed a search; hence he possessed not only the mode of the actual but also the mode of the possible. Indeed, the mere knowledge that Dasein knows that a search is possible is proof that *a priori* it knows that it is bound not only to the actual but also to the possible—hence revelation and resolution are partners in our life.[17] Binx lost his resolution when he came home, though, for he chose the wrong kind of search, became immersed in everydayness, experienced "fallenness," yet another characteristic that is innate in the human experience.[18]

On the morning of the opening of the novel Binx acknowledges that for the first time in years he had dreamed of Korea, "woke with the taste of it in my mouth, the queasy-quince taste of 1951 and the Orient" (p. 11). That taste, as he later acknowledges, is fear. Hence Binx has experienced *Befindlichkeit*, the finding of himself in a concrete placement, the strategy of introduction that Percy has repeatedly stated he employs.[19] "Opened" to experience, shocked by a catastrophe into a stunned wakefulness, Binx really looks at his world:

"this morning when I got up, I dressed as usual and began as usual to put my belongings into my pockets: wallet, notebook (for writing down occasional thoughts), pencil, keys, handkerchief, pocket slide rule (for calculating percentage returns on principal). They looked both unfamiliar and at the same time full of clues. I stood in the center of the room and gazed at the little pile, sighting through a hole made by thumb and forefinger. What was unfamiliar about them was that I could see them. They might have belonged to someone else. A man can look at this little pile on his bureau for thirty years and never once see it. It is as invisible as his own hand. Once I saw it, however, the search became possible" (p. 11).

The significance of the various objects of Binx's sight is that all are tools, implements, each of which has a specific function for him. In most cases the function is self-evident, the wallet holds his money and cards of identity, for example, but with two tools there are several possible functions to be considered, so Binx specifies (by parenthesis) their personal use. *His* notebook is for jotting down "occasional thoughts"; *his* slide rule is for the calculation of percentages. Moreover, the objects were not first perceived as indifferent things unrelated in space, then discovered to have supernumerary characteristics of specific identity, but rather were perceived as a complex of related functions, related to a unique individual. What Binx has discovered is Heidegger's tool complex, which Sartre adopts as the "relation of instrumentality,"[20] the primordial apprehension of being-in-the-world. Through his perception, Binx has realized a system of tasks that refer only to him, that represent his future; he has found himself centered in a world, even as he stands in the center of the room.

Thus Binx experiences the Sartrean "upsurge" of reflection.[21] The complex of tools has referred to a single tool which uses all the other tools. But his existence has not been established in or by an empty world; rather Binx is also the single subject who sees his objectivity while knowing that he is still a subjectivity. Thus he reflects upon a relationship that transcends the subject/object split; he is in a world by virtue of his body, no longer just in an environment as a "ghost in a machine" viewing from afar the "cinematographic representation" that he is not.

We should not, however, expect too much from Binx's upsurge of reflection. It is true that he has placed himself in his unique history after dwelling in public, that is to say, timeless, time. We should not, though, expect a basic change in his behavior, for the original reflective upsurge is in bad faith.[22] The newly reflective Binx may now be aware of himself, but he determines to remain that self by continuing his impersonation. He thinks that he can succeed in this performance because no one else is involved; the genuine reflective revolution is for-others, must be perceived by the Other. Perhaps the only change we may observe will lie not in Binx's behavior (which we know only through his not entirely trustworthy revelation), but in his narration: he should become more ironic as he expresses the essence of consciousness (reflection), which is negation: "In irony a man annihilates what he posits within one and the same act; he leads us to believe in order not to be believed; he affirms to deny and denies to affirm; he creates a positive object but it has no being other than its nothingness."[23]

Outwardly, then, Binx will continue his wandering and wondering. Inwardly, he begins a rather halfhearted search for a meaning for his life. The recognition of one's concrete placement leads to a sensitivity to the factors that determined that placement, one's "thrownness," *Geworfenheit*, as Heidegger calls it.[24] Binx begins to probe his family history, in an effort to account for his own life. On Wednesday, at his aunt's house, he studies the photographs of his father and other male relatives (pp. 24–25) and questions his aunt about them (p. 49). All he can conclude is that the older Bollings were "serene in their identities," while his father's eyes betray a trait that Binx knows all too well: "Beyond a doubt they are ironical" (p. 25).

On Thursday night Binx goes to a movie on the chance that it might enable him to achieve a repetition; noticing that a western is playing at the same theater in which he had seen *The Oxbow Incident* fourteen years before, Binx returns to it, to achieve what he avows is "a successful repetition": "the re-enactment of past experience toward the end of isolating the time segment which has lapsed in order that it, the lapsed time, can be savored of itself and without the usual adulteration of events that clog time like peanuts in brittle" (pp. 79–80). Perhaps Binx regards the experience as a success because it evoked nostalgia, which he later identifies as "the characteristic mood of repetition" (pp. 169–170), but any meaning inherent in the experience, he has to admit, "eluded" him (p. 80). Binx seems unwilling, really, to confront that life fourteen years ago, to admit that it was as fraught with everydayness as the present. In "The Man on the Train" Percy distinguishes between two forms of repetition. "The aesthetic repetition captures the savor of repetition without surrendering the self as a locus of experience and possibility," he notes, while the existential repetition is a "passionate quest in which the incident serves as a thread in the labyrinth to be followed at any cost" (*MB*, pp. 95–96). All Binx seems to experience here is the savoring of the moment, while withholding any real involvement of himself in determining to change his life. His choice of a western seems proof that he is at heart interested foremost in possibility, not actuality.

On Friday Binx devises what would at first seem to be a sincere repetition. He wishes to explore the history of the duck club, "the only relic" (p. 6) of his father that he still possesses; he would seem to want "to stand before the house of one's childhood," as Percy describes repetition in "The Man on the Train."[25] But it turns out that the whole trip to St Bernard Parish, where the club is located, is merely a part of Binx's impersonating Clark Gable in order to fascinate Sharon. Once he gets there, he contents himself to contemplate the money that he will realize from the real estate (p. 89) and to appreciate the very basic sense of ready-to-hand reality displayed by Mr. Sartalamaccia, the builder of a housing development: "I take pleasure in watching him run a thumb over the sawn edges of the sheathing" (p. 93). The conclusion of the outing emphasizes Binx's outer/inner duplicity: "I go home as the old Gable, asweat and with no thought for her and sick to death with desire" (p. 96). That "sick to death" is a nicely couched allusion to Kierkegaard's despair, the malady that really dominates Binx's private life, fueling his desire.

The weekend is dedicated to Sharon's seduction. When that achievement is frustrated, Binx seems to direct his interest to repetition, for he attempts on Sunday morning to discover from his mother something about that fellow sufferer, his dead father (pp. 148–49). But his mother has adopted a way of seeing "life, past and present, in terms of a standard comic exaggeration" (p. 151); one reduces all events to the routine—beyond that, one goes to church and fishing. With his exhaustion of both the rotational and the repetitional capacities of the weekend, Binx, not surprisingly, is overwhelmed by the malaise on the trip back to town (p. 166).

At that point in the novel, Binx becomes, literally, the man on the train. He is obliged to attend a convention in Chicago, so he and Kate, who invites herself along, take the Sieur Iberville on Sunday night. Such a jaunt is suffused with expectancy; like Thomas Wolfe before him, Binx knows "the peculiar gnosis of trains," recognizes the train as an "eminence from which there is revealed both the sorry litter of the past and the future bright and simple as can be" and also as a vehicle that facilitates zone crossing, "one's privileged progress through the world" (p. 184).

The success of rotation depends, though, upon the moviegoer's continued seclusion of himself in "unrisked possibility" or his ability to embody the stylized behavior of the stars whom he impersonates, that is, really act with gestural perfection. On the train Binx is caught in a situation in which he would like to display for Kate the sexual prowess of Clark Gable in his role as Rhett Butler. His failure is dismal, as he confesses to another of his ideals, Rory Calhoun (p. 199).[26]

But Kate, rather than fault him for his impotence, his failure to live up to his impersonation, accepts him in his reduced humanity and takes care of him (pp. 201, 202, 206). Having the night before confessed that she regarded him as the "unmoved mover" (p. 197), Kate demonstrates her faith in him as he is, and as a consequence Binx is serene in his own identity for once in his life. Thus he is free of the sexual desire that has haunted him for years as the symbol of possibility: "What an experience, Rory, to be free of it for once. Rassled out. What a sickness it is, Rory, this latter-day post-Christian sex. To be pagan it would be one thing, an easement taken easily in a rosy old pagan world; to be Christian it would be another thing, fornication forbidden and not even to be thought of in the new life, and I can see that it need not be thought of if there were such a life. But to be neither pagan nor Christian but this: oh this is a sickness, Rory" (p. 207).

Because of the love for him exhibited by Kate's taking care of him, Binx feels more of a communion, more at ease than ever before in his life. *The Young Philadelphians* (its very title suggesting agape, not eros), the movie that Binx and Kate go to see in Chicago, mirrors Binx's new found tranquillity and optimism:

> Kate holds my hand tightly in the dark.
>   Paul Newman is an idealistic young fellow who is disillusioned and becomes cynical and calculating. But in the end he recovers his ideals. (p. 211)

Such happy endings occur only in the movies, though. Both Kate and Binx emerge from the theater with a foreboding, which is fulfilled by a call from Aunt Emily, who condemns Binx's feckless behavior with Kate. Once again Binx becomes the man on the train (except that, no trains being scheduled, he is actually the man on the bus). Despite the prospect of the interview with his aunt, Binx is in reasonably good spirits. He reads *Arabia Deserta* and enjoys the sights—and watches over the sleeping Kate. His mixed activities suggest the two directions his life may take: a return to his ghostly wandering or an acceptance of the care-relation.

Part of the trip is occupied by Binx's observation of two fellow passengers, each of whom personifies an extreme of human behavior. There is, first, a romantic, a young college graduate so captivated by the ideal that he will find it extremely difficult ever to settle for the actual. Binx concludes that the romantic is "a moviegoer, though of course he does not go to the movies" (p. 216), that is, that the boy has excluded himself from the world by his very way of looking at it. There is, second, a salesman, who lives in a world of total actuality, who creates his world by the things he can touch: "he gives me a sample of his product, a simple ell of tempered and blued steel honed to a two-edged blade. Balancing it in his hand, he tests its heft and temper. The hand knows the blade, practices its own metaphysic of the goodness of the steel" (p. 216). He does not suffer any alienation at all, Binx knows, but neither does he possess any sense of the difference between himself and his environment: "Businessmen are our only metaphysicians, but the trouble is, they are one-track metaphysicians" (p. 217).[27]

When Binx stands before his aunt, he has achieved a degree of confidence that he has never before felt. But her contempt for his behavior brutally erodes the faith in himself that Kate's love had given him; Aunt Emily's last question, particularly, demonstrates her judgment: "What do you think is the purpose of life—to go to the movies and dally with every girl that comes along?" (p. 226) Binx rejects that interpretation of his character, but he can offer nothing to contradict it. Thus he stumbles off, to relapse into the very behavior his aunt had described. Thinking that Kate has seen the wisdom of her step-mother's view and therefore cast him adrift, Binx is desperate to find a woman, merge his nothingness in the only kind of being that he can enter.[28] He calls Sharon, appealing to his guardian angel for help: "I've got to find her, Rory" (p. 239). Failing to contact her, he frantically settles for her roommate Joyce, whom he tries to fascinate by impersonating Marlon Brando (p. 230). At that moment, on the verge of falling back into his most alienated form, he spies Kate, who has not betrayed him after all. They renew their intention to marry, and Binx dares to hope: "Is it possible that it is not too late?" (p. 231).

The Epilogue offers evidence of a year's success. Binx has entered medical school; thus he undertakes a genuine repetition, for he dares to resume the way of life which fatally alienated his father and which had excluded him from his own world for all of his adult life. He has remained faithful in caring for Kate, who seems to feel that she exists only because he constantly thinks of her. He mentions no movies that he has seen, nor does he affect the behavior of any movie star. Binx Bolling has come out of the movies, to chance acting himself.

NOTES

[1]In her essay "The Moviegoer of the 1950's [*Twentieth Century Literature*, 19 (July 1968), 84–89] Mary Thale emphasizes the irony that Binx cultivates to separate himself from his fellow citizens of the Eisenhower era, who have been reduced to stereotypical behavior by such media as the movies. In "Walker Percy's Indirect Communications" [*Texas Studies in Language and Literature*, 11 (Spring 1969), 867–900] I argue that Binx realizes that the movies seem to provide the kind of transcendent experience for the contemporary world that the religious institution once provided. Scott Byrd, in "Mysteries and Movies" [*Mississippi Quarterly*, 25 (Spring 1972), 165–181], discusses the references to the various movie stars in the novel, pointing out that Binx likens a person to a movie star in order to deny that person's reality and likens himself to a movie star whenever he is acting deceptively. Harvey R. Greenberg, M.D. [*The Movies on Your Mind* (New York: Saturday Review Press, 1975), p. 4], also discusses Binx's personality, approaching it from the direction of psychology: "One encounters chronic moviemania in rigid, inhibited types who feel exquisitely uncomfortable when forced into close interpersonal contact. Safe only in well-defined social situations, intolerably anxious if called upon to improvise, these people sleepwalk through the day's routine and only come alive at second hand,

as proxy participants in the adventures of their screen idols. (Walker Percy's elegant novel *The Moviegoer* describes such a case.)" More recently, Simone Vauthier, in "Title as Microtext" [*Journal of Narrative Technique*, 5 (September 1975), 219–29], has asserted that the title announces "a complex metaphor for man's ambivalent relation to experience," a generalization with great potential, but not quite sufficiently supported by analysis. The only treatment unsympathetic to the use of the moviego-ing materials is that of Alfred Kazin ["The Pilgrimage of Walker Percy," *Harper's Magazine*, 243 (June 1971), 81–86], who thinks that the title is misleading because the novel is "not exactly about going to the movies." Still, though, Kazin feels that the movie material, if it must be used, is a device that reveals Binx's basically positive nature: "He has become the one man around him who seems to want nothing for himself but to look, to be a spectator in the dark. This clinician and diagnostician of the soul trains himself in the movies. The enlarged, brilliantly lighted and concentrated figures upon the screen have taught him how to focus on the secret human places." The present essay differs with Kazin's interpretation.

2To help us understand these generalizations, Binx describes on another occasion a fellow student who had mastered the vertical search: "He was absolutely unaffected by the singularities of time and place. His abode was anywhere. It was all the same to him whether he catheterized a pig at four o'clock in the afternoon in New Orleans or at midnight in Transylvania. He was actually like one of those scientists in the movies who don't care about anything but the problem in their heads—now here is a fellow who . . . will be heard from. Yet I do not envy him. I would not change places with him if he discovered the cause and cure of cancer. For he is no more aware of the mystery which surrounds him than a fish is aware of the water it swims in. He could do research for a thousand years and never have an inkling of it" (pp. 51–52). Binx is here employing the distinction between *problem* and *mystery* made by Gabriel Marcel, in *Being and Having*, trans. Katherine Farrer, (New York: Harper and Row, 1965), pp. 100–01: "Distinguish between the Mysterious and the Problematic. A problem is something met with which bars my passage. It is before me in its entirety. A mystery, on the other hand, is something in which I find myself caught up, and whose essence is therefore not before me in its entirety. It is as though in this province the distinction between *in me* and *before me* loses its meaning.

"The Natural. The province of the Natural is the same as the province of the Problematic. We are tempted to turn mystery into problem.

"The Mysterious and Ontological are identical. There is a mystery of knowledge which belongs to the ontological order (as Maritain saw) but the epistemologist does not know this, makes a point of ignoring it, and turns it into a problem."

3Jean-Paul Sartre, *Being and Nothingness*, trans. Hazel E. Barnes, (New York: Philosophical Library, 1956), p. 200. Percy defines his relationship to Sartre in the interview with Charles T. Bunting, "An Afternoon with Walker Percy," *Notes on Mississippi Writers*, 4 (Fall 1971), 43–61.

4Sartre, p. 200.

5Sartre, p. 84.

6Sartre, pp. 176–177.

7Sartre, p. 307.

8John Carr, "Rotation and Repetition: Walker Percy," in *Kite-Flying and Other Irrational Acts* (Baton Rouge: Louisiana State Univ. Press, 1972), p. 48.

9*Partisan Review*, 23 (Fall 1956), 478–94. Reprinted in *The Message in the Bottle*.

10*The Message in the Bottle*, pp 83–100. Percy seems obviously to be alluding to Gilbert Ryle's grumpy description of the modern concern with the isolated subjectiv-ity as "the dogma of the Ghost in the Machine." See Ryle's *The Concept of Mind* (London: Hutchinson's University Library, 1949), pp. 15–16 ff, for an illustration of the "commonsense" reaction to phenomenological or existential stress on the significance of the subjective.

[11]Marcel, *Being and Having*, pp. 18–21.

[12]Sartre, pp. 59–60.

[13]Sartre, pp. 48–54.

[14]Sartre, pp. 338–39.

[15]Martin Heidegger, *Being and Time*, trans. John Macquarrie and Edward Robinson (New York: Harper and Row, 1962), pp. 179–82.

[16]Heidegger, pp. 391–96.

[17]Heidegger, pp. 182–95.

[18]Heidegger, pp. 219–24.

[19]Percy's comments on the theme of coming to oneself in a concrete place and time are found in the Abádi-Nagy, Brown, Bunting, Carr, Cremeens, and Dewey interviews and in Percy's essays, "From Facts to Fiction" and "Notes for a Novel about the End of the World."

[20]Heidegger, pp. 134–48.

[21]Sartre, p. 153.

[22]Sartre, p. 161.

[23]Sartre, p. 47.

[24]Heidegger, p. 174.

[25]*The Message in the Bottle*, p. 96. A significant point is reached in *The Last Gentleman*, when Will Barrett, having returned to the South after a sojourn in the land of the objective-empiricists, literally does stand before the house of his father.

[26]Binx's choice of Rory Calhoun, a relatively little-known movie actor, as his personification of sexual gestural perfection is explained by the revelation in *Parade* (23 October 1977, p. 1): "When actress Lita Baron bitterly divorced Rory Calhoun six years ago, she alleged that her husband had committed adultery with Betty Grable and 78 other women." Binx has apparently been a student not merely of moviegoing but also of movie goings-on.

[27]The tension between a purely abstract and a purely concrete view of the world remains the major structure of Percy's fictional world. Will Barrett is drawn between life as an engineer and life as a car dealer. Tom Moore suffers his fall because he foolishly attempts to resolve the tension between angelism and bestialism by technology. Lance Lamar, having lost the romantic-abstract view when Lucy died, opts for the concrete-genital view with Margot.

[28]The notebook of Sutter Vaught, in *The Last Gentleman*, explains much of the sexual activity that occurs or at least is thought about in Percy's novels. Sexual activity for Percy's characters is not a determined behavior (manifesting a generic energy), but a chosen behavior (manifesting an individual's desire to expand into his *en-soi*); it is more (or at least as much) a phenomenological than a physiological search.

Walker Percy and the Resonance of the Word

CHARLES P. BIGGER

> There is much that is strange, but nothing that surpasses man in strangeness.
> . . . .
> And he has found his way to the resonance of the word, and to the wind-swift all-understanding . . .
>
> Everywhere journeying, inexperienced and without issue, he comes to nothingness.
> . . . .
> Rising high above his place, he who for the sake of adventures takes the nonessent for essent loses his place in the end.
>
> Sophocles, *Antigone*, 332-72; trans. by Heidegger
> from *Introduction to Metaphysics*

In his collection of essays, *The Message in the Bottle*, Walker Percy announces his theme with "how queer man is, how queer language is, and what one has to do with the other." For Percy and for Sophocles man is strangest of all, with a strangeness (*deinon*) that is monstrous, overwhelming, violent. Man stands within the terrible power of Being, the power of the earth, the sea, the air; but his way is not to be that of the birds, the fishes, and the beasts who order themselves within and exhibit the self-restraint of Being. Man partakes in the power, the strangeness and the uncanniness of Being; but he is strange in a double sense, and thus strangest, in that his being, that of the human essent, has its *archē*, its origin (which is at the same time its governing principle) in an act of violence against the overwhelming through which he establishes himself as creator of his own order, his own justice, his own world. Man is "violence in the midst of overpowering."[1] The living totality of beings gathers itself and lays itself out as a cosmos, a harmonious order; this "self-gathering" of *physis* (nature as

43

growth, emergence from the sea and air and earth) is the original meaning of *logos*. In an original act of violence against nature man appropriates *logos* as speech so that in his "pondering and plotting" man can in his "journeyings," his rootlessness and transcendence, gather and domesticate *physis* to his ends. His order is an act of violence. But man can never domesticate his own *physis*. "The strangest (man) is what it is because, fundamentally, it cultivates and guards the familiar, only in order to break out of it and let what overpowers it break in."[2] Language (that by which man gathers into world) in its familiarity becomes another worldly instrument of power whereby man manipulates himself and others in preserving or changing a world. "Communication" becomes a relationship wherein one force "communicates" itself to another, a condition for securing effects, an event in the world. And so the world loses its strangeness and becomes a theme for technological exploitation in the hands of a science that is little more than a calculus of forces. The awe and mystery, the strangeness of Being, that induces a natural piety has given way before a methodology which can recognize only problems. With Marcel we can say that mysteries endure as the *archē* of thought; this *archē* is violated by the prevailing attitude that problems admit of solution: "Our whole attitude towards nature, our violation of nature with the help of machines and the heedless ingenuity of technicians and engineers, is hubris. . . . so is our attitude toward ourselves, upon whom we perform experiments which we would never perform on any animal, cheerfully and curiously splitting open the soul, while the body still breathes. . . . we violate ourselves, questionable questioners, as though life were nothing but a cracking of nuts."[3]

Walker Percy has, with truly remarkable success, set himself to the task of restoring strangeness to the name and to ourselves, the users of names. Just as in the novels he has celebrated, often with comic irony, the violence and strangeness of man, so too through the resonance of the name he sets himself to uncover from the banalities of the behavioral sciences the peculiar mystery of being human. While we must confess that mystery filtered through the consciousness of a Catholic Christian will have a different feel, the sense that there is a solution which is lacking in the tragic age of the Greeks, still Percy remains faithful to the natural phenomena and honest in the manner in which he articulates them.

There is a sense, however, that the price which he pays for this honesty in his philosophical reflections is too great. Percy is willing to accept many of the dogmas of naturalistic philosophy and science. In so doing he does neutralize his own Christian bias; but he sometimes tends to traffic in dead issues and to shun arguments which would make his case even more dazzling and his achievement more accessible.

That generation which came of age in the middle and late thirties and in the forties was badly served by philosophy. We were taught that intellectual respectability and sense itself lay within the modes and methods of positivistic philosophy and behavioral science and that all that was at issue in the larger world was inexplicable nonsense. To protest against that violence that raged across Europe against human order, dignity, and value was in this philosophy merely to express an emotion for which there was no empirical warrant in the protocol sentences at the base of science. These insipid trivialities, however masked by Bertie Russell's urbane wit and Freddie Ayer's rhetoric of verification, were nihilistic; we were in fact paying the price for the loss of philosophical sanity to positivism and the demonic reactions it posited. This had begun in and with the Enlightenment, and it still dominates the Western institutional life.

The only alternatives to the prevalent mythos were to be found in Neoscholasticism and Whitehead. St. Thomas could say little to the modern temper. He could indeed teach that mind has a primary intention to Being, the "first formality of the intellect," but these teachings were effective only within that German tradition that derives from Brentano and Meinong and which continues through Husserl into Heidegger and Gadamer. In the meantime Russell's famous paper "On Denoting" had virtually eliminated names and their intensional objects from Anglo-American philosophy through the legislation imposed by a formal symbolism, and there was little left to give Thomas a life of his own. Moreover, St. Thomas had little to say about the sciences of nature. The intuitions of Renaissance thinkers were correct when they replaced classification by measurement and found in Plato, rather than Aristotle, a satisfactory heuristic for science. Whitehead certainly presented a more satisfactory option. Even though he had served the establishment well with his logic, he remained an outsider. His terminology simply put people off; his breadth of vision was far too wide for a race of meditative moles. Some other age beyond this sad Alexandrian era will recognize him for what he was, the most splendid product of our tradition since Hegel, perhaps even the Greeks.

Walker Percy is a colonial thinker. The territory he inhabits received its charter for exploration from the established order as it existed when he was in fact a student member of the academic community; and as a colonial he has explored his territory from this perspective. His medical and scientific training certainly disposed him to regard the sciences as eminently respectable. Indeed, I think that as a novelist he feels that he is dealing with a frivolous genre, with something slightly suspect which does not befit the concern of a serious and public-spirited Christian gentleman. Perhaps for these reasons Percy has permitted himself a certain lack of restraint; guilt, we know, does indeed justify unacceptable practice. And so the novels celebrate human strangeness—"how queer man is."

We know that Walker Percy as a writer has been powerfully influenced by the work of Kierkegaard, Sartre, Camus, and other literature of alienation. There is perhaps a story to be told of how his remarkable vision of human strangeness was won through suffering against his own scientistic roots, even if these had been nourished in his youth by considerable personal contact with writers. When existentialism became a fashion in some literary circles after the war, we who were enemies of positivism had been so conditioned by its ascetic rigors that it was dismissed as a disease of the Cartesian *res cogito*. Philosophy had to share the objectivity of science, uncontaminated by consciousness and its idiosyncratic points of view and other such manifest historical contingencies. What Percy could do in the novel was forbidden in philosophy. But a denial of phenomenological existentialism as a base for philosophy had other reasons. Percy had been reading St. Thomas and saw that the dignity of the epistemological enterprise, man's primordial intention to Being, was lost in philosophies that seemed to be replaying Cartesian themes. Idealism, even if it is able to gather up much that is distinctively human, lacked in its solipsistic tendencies that incarnate sense of the "word made flesh." Percy saw that his task in reflecting on the word lay between the space-time events of naturalism and the alienated realms of spirit, that it was a task of pairing, of reconciliation. For Aquinas, the mind is apportioned towards things. To this harmony of the concept and the thing Percy adds a new dimension: the resonances between words and things and between these formal signs themselves makes possible knowing and human community. In the resonance one grasps identities (the essence of the thing and the self of the other) through otherness. This is the "all understanding" that lies at the roots of the soul's power to transcend environment and to have world, to play at being God.

Naming is that act which at once denotes and asserts, which pairs a phoneme (or grapheme) with something in the world in an ineluctible bond of intentional identity. It is the event that makes possible world. That mystery is best understood in its absence and subsequent eruption into world; the naming event is both a call by Being and a violence against Being. In naming, a pairing of the vocable and the things demonstrated, we constitute a common horizon with another and an opening on Being in which beings can show and make manifest themselves. But that act is itself against that power whereby beings causally communicate with one another; it is a trancendence of persons to world so that we can apprehend the truth about the world. These are the themes, born from despair, and nothing more noble and splendid has been born from the rag and bone shop of the human heart and mind than Percy's response to this calling.[4]

The canons of intellectual respectabililty are looser these days in philosophy, and much has been done of late that would make Percy's task easier. Before we look at the mode and manner of current concern, we might notice one important benefit that follows from Percy's provincialism. Hans Jonas has argued that materialism is less hospitable to the human spirit than idealism. The latter has the unwholesome habit of drinking up and including within itself every phenomenon which might be hostile to itself. It therefore has the disarming quality of an ideology rather than the falsifiability of ordinary scientific knowledge. That which explains everything explains nothing. If one

begins with materialism and tries to understand mind, there is at least
the possibility of finding what is uniquely and irreducibly mental. If
we try to place language within the forms of the spirit we are never
likely to discover what is strange and unique to language. If we begin
with the absence of language and the attempts to explain it as a natural
phenomenon, as an event in the world rather than as the transcendental condition for the possibility of both its own empirical reality and
world, then we are more likely to catch language in its unique reality,
which is transcendental.

A sign is that which provokes some response in a being towards an
object or state of affairs with which that sign is "associated." Signs are
causes, but what they effect is relation to another. Their causality is in
virtue of their significance: a red sign causes us to stop, not because it
is red, but rather because it means "stop," and this meaning or connection between the sign and the thing signified is established by habit
formation. The neural and physical events associated with seeing red
and coming to a stop belong to ordinary physical and physiological
theory. The unique relation of signification is behavioral and belongs
to psychology. In conditioning theory, learning language is learning
relations of significance between more or less arbitrary signs and the
appropriate behavioral response. Semantics is concerned with these
relations of significance. But syntactics is a formal science, since it has
to do with the order of categorematic and syncategorematic signs in
sentences. The odd feature about syntax is that linguistic competence
permits an indefinite freedom in syntactical formation that is out of
keeping with the stimulus input into the system: there is no way of
accounting behaviorly for what a very young child can do with the
syntax of language. At this point structuralism appears upon the scene
with its claim to an *a priori* syntactical competence. The mechanism
of word learning is confronted with a human capacity that seems to
defy *a posteriori* mechanical explanation. This is the battle that has
been joined between Skinner and Chomsky. Percy finds in names a
middle ground that is empirical and that meets the requirement of
rational structure.

Walker Percy seems to feel that behaviorism is essentially right-
headed in its insistence that animal behavior is to be understood
within the nomological rubric of lawlike sequence; and this is the

general pattern of scientific explanation. In conceding this case for the lower animals, Percy may be granting too much. What won't work in bacteria is unlikely to be true at the level of dogs and cats. In abandoning the lower forms to mechanism and leaving language to man, are we not embracing that very Cartesianism that is elsewhere so violently denied? Animals are not mechanisms.[5] Virtually every school of recent philosophy has converged to dislodge positivism and mechanism from the theory of action. Intentionality and teleology are now at least as respectable as mechanism. Behaviorism is virtually a dead issue, and its theory of language is as quaint as Aristotle's view of the mechanics of the solar system.

If we grant Percy classical learning theory, we then see with him that we cannot account for truth. Truth is an assertion that something shows itself as something. Truth may involve all sorts of physical and psychological processes: but a process is just what it is, while an assertion is (with the rest of language) a normative claim that can be false or otherwise inappropriate. We may hold a man responsible for shooting a gun, not for the processes that produce death. A stimulus-response process can in itself only be described: its evaluation belongs to that structure of intentions, to meaning and truth, whose ends it is invoked to serve. Langauge may be an event in the world, but it strangely transcends that world in bringing itself and world to judgment. As Kant would say, language is a transcendental condition for its own empirical possibility as a structure of communication events. That is our strangeness.

The simplest element of language is the name; the implicit *is* of the naming act constitutes an intentional unity between the name and its object, asserting of that object when it is grasped through the transparency of the name that it is a member of a type or kind. The vocal or graphic sign, as well as the painting or the dance, becomes through assertion a symbol in which being is apprehended as something or other. The savage and the child grasp the power of names to bring to presence things. The symbol makes present world. *For once we begin to name, everything has a name. The world becomes a totality, wholly grasped and domesticated by the resonant word.* Animals have an environment made up of objects of potential interest. An environment has gaps. When Helen Keller recognized that the marks Miss Sullivan

was making on her hand symbolized the water that wet them, she
knew that everything had a name, that world is a totality of meaning
and significance.

Roman Jakobson reminds us that modern linguistics owes its origins to Husserl's *Logical Investigations*. The idea of a pure grammar
was superimposed on "the exclusively empiric grammar which at that
time was the only one accepted."[6] In the sense of Kant and Husserl, to
be "pure" or "a priori" is to be repeatable (and thus formal) in an act
that is transparent to itself. In this sense, the *a priori* is something that
is a condition for self-responsibility, something that is authentically
mine. A mere belief, for instance, is something that "they" deliver,
something that I now hold in accord with the fashions "they" set and
abandon when "they" abandon it too. Husserl was concerned to
secure for man the humanistic ideal, the ideal of authentic self-
responsible rationality, against the threats of naturalism. He believed
that we can overcome naturalism only if we return to "the things
themselves" in a resolute effort to describe them in their appearing.
Naturalism is the "loss of the creature" to the essentially reductive
categories and concepts of the paradigmatic physical sciences. What
appears in its appearing is always a case of this or that, an instance or a
kind. Materialism drinks dry the springs of meaning and value, the
power of poetry to engender vision, the reality of relations between
autonomous persons, such as the love of man for man and for God. The
autonomous foundations of the spirit, the domain of culture and its
justification by Goodness and Beauty, become epiphenomena of a
blind and senseless clash of matter. The *epoche* frees us from the
standpoint of naturalism and lets us encounter things as meant in
something close to their unprejudiced reality. While there is much to
be said against this project and the way in which it was carried out by
Husserl himself, his insistence on an evidential basis for thought and
his search for the unprejudiced so that beings could be released into
their full reality was not an ignoble enterprise. Husserl's idea of a
universal grammar should be viewed in this light. Walker Percy is far
closer to Husserl than he realizes, and this is to the good. He indeed
carries Husserl's program for a pure grammar a big step forward by
avoiding the solipsism of idealism. Since the virtuality of a signification was for Husserl equivalent to its reality, he failed to grasp the role

of radical otherness in language. Percy's concept of pairing does respect this otherness and enables us to define a world in ways quite compatible with realism.

Walker Percy is suspicious of the phenomenological sense of world, for rightly he fears that solipsistic form through which it manifests itself in Husserl. Things are not merely meanings. But the phenomenological concept of world as horizon is not incompatible with the transcendental realism that Percy advances in his theory of names. It is indeed a useful means of understanding and illuminating his account of the possibility of language and, above all, the role of metaphor. An horizon is that opening, that clearing, in which beings can show themselves meaningfully. As transcendental it is the *a priori* condition, disclosed in Helen Keller's discovery of names, for the unitary appearance of beings founded on the mind's intention to Being, through other beings, the signifiers. This is an eidetic necessity, not a matter of contingent fact. Naming is a process of distantiation and objectification, the abstraction from the general flux of events of something or other as determinately this or that. The pairing of word and things and word with word (identificatory and apophanic judgment) brings before us beings in their formal and material relations with other beings. This pairing is the transcendental condition for world, the possibility of a horizon in which things can show themselves in manifold manners of relatedness and connexity, real and ideal. It is a realistic analogue of Kant's categories of the understanding. Moreover, naming is always for another, even for ourselves in our temporal otherness. The iterative structure of sensible signifiers is the realistic condition for language, our capacity to pair the hetrogeneous. Naming requires an other who receives what we demonstrate and describe through marks and sounds.[7] The name must be given in authority and good faith. The effectiveness of a name is a function of its opacity, its lack of descriptive and ikonic force. When I name water as *water*, through the implicit *is*, I raise this unique event to the level of the universal; for I say what this *is*. The intention to Being is that of formulable *quidditas*. This is the great scholastic point that Heidegger has done so much to refurbish.

Language as the opening of the horizon for the appearance of beings is, in virtue of the formulable essences (the nominalizing force of the

Greek *einai, to be*) that appear through the name, also a power against Being, a power that reduces emergences and Becoming to the stasis of logic and theory. In its proper Greek sense, *theoria* is presence at a sacred spectacle in which there is a plenary manifestation of Being, a breaking through into unconcealment, *aletheia* (truth). In *theoria* we encounter strangeness. Theory in the hands of the practicing scientist is a means of participatory observation, of being present with the object in the event of its unconcealment (participation) and of that distantiation (observation) that is a reflective and analytic assessment of what is revealed. This is the theme of Percy's several marvelous discussions of psychiatric practice. In this participatory context, which involves action, what is manifest in essence is the entity's mode and manner of operation, the potential of the entity to act and undergo. This is a scholastic point. But when theory comes to have the layman's sense, and I am afraid that most philosophers of science are in this sense layman, then "formulable essence" means the potentiality of the term for formal analysis, for logical proof and archetypal reality. Concepts now preempt the agent of his sovereignty over his own experience, and we are faced with the "loss of the creature." Nature is denatured. The world becomes a collection of dead objects ordered to and by theory. Language further alienates in that we give a concreteness to our abstractions which is in turn denied to the real concreteness of living experience. Percy has read his Whitehead. The formal, the expert's presumed knowledge of theory (something that he is supposed to have rather than be) determines experience as its paradigmatic criterion. Everything is a case or an instance. This is nowhere more elegantly exploited than in Percy's critique of the formalism of Chomsky's theory of innate grammar. Percy shows that this theory cannot be a theory of grammar by its own criterion of theory; furthermore, all the theory we need about syntax can be derived from that participation involved in learning language. *Theoria* underlies theory.

The context of naming is the context of living speech, of the word that gives life to world. The fundamental pairing between the world of objects and sensible signs is the prototype for the development of syntax and its structures. The text concludes with this alternative to Chomsky. Since naming is not an empirical contingency, an event in the world, the structure discerned in this pairing is rational and metaphysical. The assertion involved in this identificatory judgment (pairing), the water that is *water*, is extended to that pairing which is the apophanic judgment, the relation between symbols, S is P. The thing/word is transformed in language learning to the word/word. Percy then proposes and gives evidence that this structure is sufficient to do the work of Chomsky's "language acquisition device." Does it work? If it does, it is a contribution of considerable importance to formal linguistics. I will leave to those who have a better feel for *theoria* and theory than I the task of criticism.

Perhaps the most interesting contribution to our understanding of language lies in Percy's analysis of mistaken metaphor. I shall not explore this topic in this context. Let me say that if we put this together with the recent discussions of the role of metaphor in the philosophy of science by Max Black and Mary Hesse, and if we exploit the concept of world as horizon, we then have the grounds for a genuinely radical revision in our conceptual systems. Metaphor is another case of pairing, one wherein two structures are revealed through names that interpret each other and thereby open a horizon for a recovery of beings¯ in their beingness and meaningfulness. Metaphor is an *epoche¯,* one that releases world from the stale and sedimented habits of language and lets the strange appear in its strangeness. Through metaphor we recover the creature and the full mystery of the resonance of the word.

Percy once said that he wrote novels when he got philosophical cramps. One can say that his philosophy cures many philosophical cramps. By centering on one point, the mystery of naming as disclosing world, Percy has performed a remarkable service towards our recovery of strangeness. We take world as a fact, as a given. But "world" as such has its origin in myth. The concept of world presupposed in any segmentation is *a priori*. It can hardly be an inductive, empirical concept. What was given by language about the gods now appears as the correlative of language itself. To speak of world as a totality of structures of meaning and value embracing relations to self, to others and to nature is to adopt the view of a god. The possibility of language discloses us as beings within and without the world. This is very strange indeed. Worlds can be lost. On the one hand they can be lost to the nihilism of naturalism. On the other hand, they can be sublimated into the formations of self or language. Percy retains the tension and lets the mystery show itself. Is this not very close to an incarnational theology?

NOTES

[1]Martin Heidegger, *Introduction to Metaphysics* (New Haven: Yale Univ. Press, 1961), pp. 123–38 is an indispensable text for getting right about Walker Percy, the novelist and philosopher. For further elucidation of *deinon*, see Hans-Georg Gadamer, *Truth and Method* (New York: Seabury Press, 1975), p. 289 and Aristotle, *Eth. Nic.*, 1144a 23ff.

[2]Heidegger, p. 137.

[3]Nietzsche, *Genealogy of Morals*, III, 9.

[4]Unfortunately Percy does not consider the case of proper names. His names are always class designators, and so Russell semantics is not so much dealt with as sidestepped. But one of the most important recent contributions in the republic of letters is addressed to this problem; Saul Kripke's account of naming and essence is quite in keeping with Percy's belief that naming is irreducible. Kripke shows that naming does not reduce to description, to truth, functional statements with predicate constants. There are a number of technical problems one could raise against Percy, but then problems can be solved with sufficient ingenuity. Problems are usually raised to quash inquiry and to create an artificial consensus, for most of us do not have the wit to solve problems that really lie in the techniques of presentation. Basic conceptual insights are often abandoned in the face of the necessity of conforming to some ritual practice.

[5]Bacteria and animals, like men, are self-interpreting beings operating at the level of meanings, not causes, and this is true even at the molecular level of life. See Bigger and Bigger, "DNA Integrity: A Non-Reductive Chemistry of Life," *Proceedings of the 16th International Congress of Philosophy* (Dusseldorf, 1978), pp. 91–3. Of the greatest importance is Hans Jonas, *The Phenomenon of Life* (New York: Dell, 1966).

[6]*Main Trends in the Science of Language*, (New York, 1974), p. 13.

[7]Additional support for this public view of language is to be found in Jacques Derrida's critique of Husserl's theory of signs in *Speech and Phenomena* (Evanston: Northwestern Univ. Press, 1973) and in Wittgenstein's argument against a private language in his *Investigations*.

Art as Symbolic Action:
Walker Percy's Aesthetic

MICHAEL PEARSON

The novelist is less like a prophet than he is like a canary that the coal miners used to take down into the shaft to test the air. When the canary gets unhappy, utters plaintive cries, and collapses, it may be time for the miners to surface and think things over. (*MB*, p. 101)

In *The Message in the Bottle* Walker Percy offers what he terms a general philosophical anthropology, an effort at cognition in an age where reality is distorted. For Percy, a careful look at language will point toward a clearer image of the human condition. All of his theories—linguistic, philosophical, and aesthetic—hinge on the central concept of symbolization. The rib of theory, beginning with the linguistic premises and building to the aesthetic beliefs, springs dramatically to life in his novels.

The germ of Percy's aesthetic theory begins with his disagreement with the behavioristic thesis that language can be explained as a stimulus-response mechanism. The flaw in the behavioristic thesis is that it makes no distinction between a sign and a symbol. With a sign comes a response, attention being directed toward an object. If we say *stick* to a trained dog, he will fetch it. On the other hand, a fellow human will (possibly) wait politely and eventually say, "What about it?" A sign is a directive to act; a symbol is a vehicle for thought. A symbol, as Percy says, "somehow comes to contain within itself the thing it means." Naming sets human language apart from other forms of animal communication; it embodies what Milton called a "sudden apprehension" of something.

Close to Percy's own viewpoint is Chomsky's conception of human language as entirely different from communication in other species. However, instead of explaining the mystery, the transformationalists restate the problem. As recent critics have pointed out, Percy does much the same.[1] But he does so for a different reason. It is his purpose to take apart the theories of man as a mechanism to be explained, but at the same time he never allows his theoretical roamings to leave the realm of the individual, how he uses language and how it affects his way of knowing. Percy realizes that his "theory" (rather a "description") of language will not unlock the mysteries of symbolization, but his ideas might, as he suggests, open up new ways of thinking about them.

Percy's own language theories come in part from a realization he came to while thinking about an incident in the life of Helen Keller. It may be reasonable to conclude that Percy's initial interest in language flows from a more personal source: his discovery that his daughter Ann had been born deaf. It is, however, Miss Keller's language breakthrough that Percy consistently draws upon to support his own ideas. As he explains, prior to her discovery, Helen understood the word *water* (any word, for that matter) only as a sign; she would respond to the word by bringing a jug or drinking a cup of water, but during her naming experience, the word *water* denoted the substance itself. The name became a way of knowing the thing, not merely a way of responding to it. There are three elements involved in Helen's awakening to language: Helen, the water, and the word *water*. Percy asks: "But how? What was the base of the triangle? What is the nature of the mysterious event in which one perceives that *this* (stuff) 'is' *water*?" (*MB*, p. 40).

Symbolization is the specifically human activity. Science tells us how we are like other organisms or how we resemble other individuals, but it does not deal with the uniqueness of symbolization. Percy refuses to accept the post-Darwinian idea of man as a higher grade in the class of animals. Instead, man is an animal that must be placed in a separate class. As Kierkegaard said, "What man is cannot be grasped by the sciences of man." Rather than accept the scientific recipe for human-ness, Percy wishes to join his scientific training with the existentialist tradition. Avoiding an "allegiance to a theoretical commitment," he wants to observe carefully, to discover and describe how an individual speaks, acts, and feels in a given situation. A study of symbolization, Percy believes, should provide the bridge to connect writer and scientist. Both can examine the symbolic transformation, "the unique and universal human response." Following Suzanne Langer's suggestion in *Philosophy in a New Key*, Percy claims that we can no longer ignore the importance of the symbolic process, the act of communication, of "making common." Nor can we ignore the fact that the misuse and abuse of symbolization have been part of the cause of the spiritual atrophy in modern man.

In his essay "The Loss of the Creature" Percy cogently describes man's plight in contemporary technological society. With the novelist's skill, he uses a series of anecdotes to detail the fact that modern man has lost or abdicated his sovereignty as a knower. The experts from the media, the sciences, the universities, and other hallowed grounds have appropriated the ways of knowing. A more radical epistemology, then, is called for. Although few people are able to see things in their pristine state, men should, according to Percy, assume the posture of Crusoe seeing the footprint on the beach. Crusoe, a favorite image for Percy, is the paradigm of the sovereign individual, a castaway who can actually acknowledge existence on his own terms. Too often man cannot see beyond the packaging of an experience, creating a situation where the frog becomes the specimen, the sonnet becomes the educational wrapping, the Negro becomes an example of some sociological trait.

Before a man begins his search for sovereignty, he must recognize his condition for what it is. Percy's epigraph for *The Moviegoer* from Kierkegaard's *The Sickness Unto Death* (". . . the specific character of despair is precisely this: it is unaware of being despair") points to the belief that one must be conscious of his predicament before beginning any quest. As Percy dramatized in *Love in the Ruins*, consensus wisdom has become an obstacle to genuine naming and when the barriers to communication become too great, man is left in despair. The symbol can alienate us from people and environment or it can bring us into the neighborhood of being. Language is a social act, and it can be an intersubjective process. We name something for ourselves and for someone else, even if that someone is an implied "I." As Sarah Henisey has pointed out, "Intersubjectivity provides one with another unformulable person with whom he may hold communion. In this way intersubjectivity cures alienation."[2] Human language suggests a participation, a union of selves. In Percy's words: "The presence of the two organisms is not merely a genetic requirement, a *sine qua non* of symbolization; it is rather its enduring condition, its indispensable climate. Every act of symbolization, a naming, a forming an hypothesis, creating a line of poetry, perhaps even thinking, implies *another* as a co-conceiver, a co-celebrant of the thing which is symbolized" (*MB*, p. 257).

Not many writers would even think of using the word *co-celebrant* in this context. The word itself suggests the sacredness of the individual and the affirmatory potential of the symbolic exchange. When a man loses his ability or his desire to communicate with his fellowman, the malaise settles like fall-out, and he becomes a solipsist *malgré lui*. What Marcel would call the "intersubjective milieu" turns into the debilitating relationship that Buber describes as the "I-it." As Sam Keen phrases it, "As the capacity to love, to admire, and to hope dries up, the functional man loses his ability, and even the desire to transcend his situation of alienation and captivity. His world loses its mysterious character. . . . all things are explained by reference to the categories of cause and effect."[3]

Although certainly offering no panacea, Percy the novelist enters here, for it is through its re-presentation that alienation can be reversed. Reader and author can be co-celebrants in the new symbol, the work of art. In the philosophical sense, the artist and the reader may share the joy of recognizing a plight in common. Similar to Percy, Kenneth Burke stresses that language is a type of action, "symbolic action—and its nature is such that it can be used as a tool."[4] A tool, of course, can be used for a variety of purposes, good or bad. Percy's aesthetic derives from the hope that we can use language as a tool for knowledge and survival. Language, particularly in the aesthetic sphere of art, is not an instrument for cause and effect; however, it can stimulate a new awareness, a symbolic action.

It is Percy's hope that literature can be "news," the message that will deliver man from despair. For Percy, the "news" is the Christian, specifically Catholic, message, but Percy is also attempting to renew faith in man as a sovereign knower in a universe of experience. Literature is one of our instruments for knowing. It does not eradicate alienation, but it does place us in a position to recognize despair and its cause. Percy does not view literature as a means to an end, but as an articulation of the previously unnamed. It is the known but unspoken put into words. Literature, like metaphor in general, is a way of knowing. It is, as Percy has asserted, "primarily cognitive. . . . what is transmitted primarily is not feelings but the forms of feelings and that involves the act of cognition."[5]

It is the place of true art to recapture, to rename, the details of human experience, helping us to know the actual nature of our existence. Art, for Percy, is a type of "verification which takes the form of recognition. . . . the main thing that happens and the main source of pleasure in the reader is a sense of recognizing something, something that he knew, but which has been verified to him and affirmed for him by the writer."[6] This verification is cognitive because it is not merely a stimulus-response transaction or just a transmission of feelings; it is a naming, a way of seeing something.

In more traditional terms, Percy's theory of art is essentially mimetic: the reference of the work of art to the subject matter is primary. Art imitates man's true status in the universe. Percy uses the novel to unite empirical practice with existentialist perception. His fiction approximates reality in wise and startling ways, but each novel describes a particular man in a specific situation. It is one central consciousness (Binx, Will, Tom, or Lance) that Percy focuses on, but the author takes the word *consciousness* back to its origins—"a knowing with others." For this reason, the dialogue in Percy's novels is extremely important. The characters' words, more than their actions at times, tell us who they are, what their problems are, and where they are heading. Language is an observable phenomenon, and Percy is committed to an empirical analysis of this extraordinary and specifically human action. He scrutinizes the uses and abuses of language, for he is interested in the individual man, how language affects his ability to understand himself and the world around him. Particularly through the dialogue in his novels, he reminds the reader that consciousness and intersubjectivity are inextricably linked. One knows through the mirror of language, and language is a social participation. It is through the pairing of the symbol with the object that reality is fixed. The symbol, asserting an identity between name and thing, also attests to a relationship between namer and hearer. Naming creates a bond, two people becoming co-conceivers of an object under the auspices of the same symbol. Symbolization, in this respect, is an affirmation.

In a letter to me,[7] Walker Percy offered some helpful suggestions for understanding his concept of the relationship between the work of art and the world. Like all authentic symbolization, literature is intersubjective. Percy, a man with a penchant for diagrams, included one in his letter:

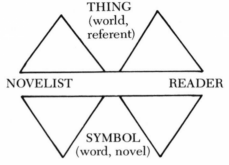

Percy's diagram is valuable because it returns two possible parameters: the relationship between novelist and reader, and the one between novel and world. The novelist and the reader may enjoy an intersubjective encounter, a two-way street: how the novelist envisions his reader and how the reader receives the novelist. In his letter Percy explains the diagram as follows: "The relation of identity between symbol (novel) and thing (world) depicted is a normative continuum allowing for the discovering and confirming effect of good art at one pole and the concealing, boring simulacrum of bad art or worn-out symbols at the opposite pole."

Novelist recaptures reality, reader re-experiences it. The vocation of the artist is to "create new language by way of metaphor."[8] Both are

involved in naming, the novelist in creating new metaphors to represent experience and the reader in devising new strategies for
re-understanding the symbol and the world. The novelist creates what
Kenneth Burke would call "prophesies after the event."

Percy's books are studies of man's inability to speak to his fellowman, and affirmations of man's potential to communicate, to be fully
human. In *The Moviegoer* we are given a carefully modulated satirical
tone; the final affirmation of the novel is oblique. The reader is forced
to watch, interpret, and understand the encounter between Binx and
Kate. It is the dialogue between them that is salient in the final pages.
We as readers observe the naming activity. Likewise, *The Last Gentleman* ends with a conversation between Sutter and Will. Again,
Love in the Ruins concludes with the simple words passing between
Tom and Ellen.[9] In his first three novels, Percy asks the reader to view
the mystery of language, to see that it can screen the world from sight
or it can be a lens to clarify reality. He does not attempt to "edify" but
to re-present.

In *Lancelot* Percy pushes the reader even more forcibly into the
symbolic process. In a conversation with Martin Luschei, Percy said
that his first three novels constituted a group and that "he would never
write another like them."[10] Although typically Percyan characters and
themes emerge in *Lancelot*, the novel is a departure from his other
works. Given his language theory, philosophical concerns, and
aesthetic beliefs, *Lancelot* was an idea whose time had come. For
Percy, art is an accurate re-presentation of life, and language is the
specifically human act; therefore, it is logical that he would center the
most important scenes in his novels upon the dialogue. In *Lancelot*,
Percy creates a monologue, thereby emphasizing the fact that all is
symbolic action. He is no longer satisfied, it seems, with the reader's
viewing genuine naming between two characters. Now, Percy beck-
ons the reader to enter into the ordeal of naming. *Lancelot* becomes a
dialogue between the main character and the reader, who is called
upon to respond to Lancelot's viewpoint. The reader, like Percival, is a
participant in the narrative. The silence, which gathers force and ends
with the final *yes*, engages the listener-reader and insists that he find
an alternative to Lancelot's eloquently mad viewpoint. The reader

must become an aggressive listener, one who will examine and challenge Lancelot's method and motive. The silence is a lacuna that increasingly begs to be filled.

Again, as in the first three novels, Percy describes the emptiness of faddish institutionalized searching, the wrongness of allowing experts to certify reality, and the alienation caused by a misuse of language. But this time he has drawn the battle lines a bit tighter: the Southern Stoic versus the traditional Christian. Percy's eloquent Stoics, both Aunt Emily and Lancelot, are modeled to a large extent on William Alexander Percy. However, it is a critical mistake to see the Stoics as a chorus for Walker Percy's own point of view. It is misinformed to say, as one critic has, that "Lance, or Percy, has had a craw full of the ethics of life adjustment."[11] True, Percy and Lancelot seem to hold many ideas in common, but one should not assume from this that "The code has become a part of Southern mores; it has become a part of Percy."[12] As Cleanth Brooks recently suggested, Lancelot, unlike Percy, has "a Gnostic impatience with human limitations . . . an amoral disregard for ethical systems demanding decency in the human community."[13] Whether we regard Lancelot as a modern Gnostic, as Brooks does, or as a secular humanist, as Robert D. Daniel does, we must realize that Percy (and the reader) are forever separated from Lancelot by a wide reach of morality. As Daniel points out, "Lancelot's claim to be a prophet unwilling to tolerate the sins of his age is undermined by our realization that he is its 'finest' product."[14] He fits well into an age that has produced Charles Manson and David Berkowitz. All three had "missions" and are incapable of feeling guilt. Stoicism and Gnosticism run counter to Christianity and to Percy's theory of language as a sharing, as a knowing *with* others. Lancelot, however, has ruled others out. He decides that " 'Evil' is surely the clue to this age, the only quest appropriate to the age. For everything and everyone's either wonderful or sick and nothing is evil" (*L*, p. 138). For the "Knight of the Unholy Grail," as for the Stoic, evil is the key to the mysteries of the age. Lance, however, never sees the evil that is closest at hand, his own inability to love.

Near the conclusion of the novel, the Stoic and Christian viewpoints clash dramatically. "Friday Afternoon at the Movies" begins with Lance's viewing the "actors" in his *cinéma vérité*. Because of the flaw in Elgin's camera, the people in the film appear to be tiny reddish figurines, like people in a darkroom. They seem to "meet, merge, and flow through each other. Lights and darks were reversed like a negative, mouths opened on light, eyes were white sockets" (*L*, p. 185). It is a ghastly picture, with people appearing to be blown in an electric wind, pieces of bodies flying around. However, for the Stoic seeking revenge this is the serendipitous distortion: Lancelot's strange view of the individuals allows him to forget their human qualities. Referring to Margot as "It" and speaking of "extended pseudopods," Lance is guilty of the same misuse of language that other characters in the novel commit. For example, in a conversation with Lance just before the violent conclusion, Margot tells him: "I love you as I've always loved you, with the old me. But there are other me's. One grows" (*L*, p. 207). Beginning with the first person pronoun, Margot uses a metaphorical sleight-of-hand to trail off into using a third person pronoun. There is no "I," there is no responsibility. Language becomes a thing to hide behind. In a similar vein, Lance describes Margot and Jacoby in bed: "Though I must have been leaning, I seemed to be floating over them. Jacoby's back was a darkness within the dark. Musingly I touched it, the beast" (*L*, p. 239). From "them" to "it," Margot and Jacoby have been turned into the two-headed Janus, one side youthful and the other aged. It is easy, then, for Lancelot to end the beast's life without any regrets. After all, it is a beast, not human beings. In the words of Philip Marlowe, an archetypal seeker of truth and Stoic like Lamar, Lancelot has become "as hollow and empty as the spaces between the stars."

With *Lancelot*, it seems that Percy is no longer content with the reader's viewing genuine naming between two characters. Now, Percy presses the reader to enter into the struggle to name his own experience. Some readers have felt that Percy should present his own viewpoint in *Lancelot* and not disappear in a rush of syllables at the end. Whether he is totally successful or not in his fourth novel, Percy is attempting to create an intersubjective moment, one in which the reader must take action, a symbolic action, that is. He is attempting, it seems, to describe the vocation of the reader, one who enters into the ordeal of naming. Percy's words, in *Lancelot* and his other novels, help us to see afresh, to recapture a world that has slipped away through inattention. *Lancelot* literally creates a listener who must turn speaker or accept the implications of the final silence.

NOTES

[1] Panthea Broughton, ed., *The Art of Walker Percy: Stratagems for Being* (Baton Rouge: Louisiana State Univ. Press, 1979), pp. 169–218. Both Weldon Thornton and William H. Poteat analyze Percy's language theories.

[2] Sarah Henisey, "Intersubjectivity in Symbolization," *Renascence*, 20 (Summer 1968), p. 210.

[3] Sam Keen, *Gabriel Marcel* (Richmond: John Knox Press, 1967), p. 10.

[4] Kenneth Burke, *Language as Symbolic Action* (Berkeley and Los Angeles: University of California Press, 1966), p. 15.

[5] Walker Percy, "A Symposium on Fiction," *Shenandoah*, 27 (Winter 1976), p. 4.

[6] Ibid., p. 11.

[7] Letter from Walker Percy to Michael Pearson dated 25 May 1976.

[8] Percy in *Shenandoah*, p. 20.

[9] In a relatively uncomplicated computer analysis of the first and last sections of the novel, I discovered that there are few present participles in the opening (7/245—roughly 2% of the total words); whereas, in the conclusion, Percy uses considerably more (17/275—approximately 7%). On the other hand, Percy uses many more past participles in the first section than he does in the last section (10 to 1 respectively). The novel, as this suggests, begins in an atmosphere of past-ness, a sense of things lost, but it ends in an ambiance of immediacy, a present regained, a fresh beginning.

The connotations of the past and present participles are also illuminating. In the opening part of his novel, Percy employs present participles with negative associations, words dealing with the end (death-dealing, Christ-forgetting) or with an almost-physical reaction to despair (jerking). In the last part of *Love in the Ruins*, the participles point to things more positive and more tangible (barbecuing, dancing, fetching, fixing, singing). The contrast in word choice is a reflection of Percy's message. Spiritual renewal, evoked by the immediacy of present participles in the last chapter, is communicated by style as well as meaning. Also, the use of words that have a direct correspondence with the things that they are naming (as opposed to the more abstract terms in the first chapter) emphasizes a specific use of language. Style, then, becomes more than a carrier of meaning. It becomes meaning itself.

[10] Martin Luschei, *The Sovereign Wayfarer: Walker Percy's Diagnosis of the Malaise* (Baton Rouge: Louisiana State Univ. Press, 1972), p. 241.

[11] Edward J. Cashin, "History as Mores: Walker Percy's *Lancelot*," *Georgia Review*, 31 (Winter 1977), p. 879.

[12] Ibid., p. 879.

[13] Cleanth Brooks, "Walker Percy and Modern Gnosticism," *The Southern Review*, 13 (Autumn 1977), p. 685.

[14] Robert D. Daniel, "Walker Percy's Lancelot: Secular Raving and Religious Silence," *The Southern Review*, 14 (Winter 1978), p. 189.

Charles Peirce and Walker Percy:
From Semiotic to Narrative

J. P. TELOTTE

Walker Percy seems almost an anomaly among modern writers, for he has been so willing to acknowledge and discuss his indebtedness to others—both fellow novelists and philosophers—as to subvert any claim to originality. While this openness has permitted his readers to more easily trace out the influences of figures like Sartre, Kierkegaard, and Dostoevsky on his work, it has also often resulted in an imbalanced reading of his novels. In many cases they have been approached solely from this philosophical perspective or treated simply as American variations on the genus "European existential novel." With the publication of his collected linguistic essays in *The Message in the Bottle*, though, two important points have emerged: 1) since they incorporate his existential views, Percy's linguistic theories may afford a new, more comprehensive approach to his fiction; and 2) because the main influence on his linguistics is the American philosopher Charles Sanders Peirce,[1] a fruitful revaluation might properly begin from that native perspective which Peirce's semiotic work provides. In this essay I wish to describe Percy's adaptations of Peirce's semiotics and suggest what implications this linguistic concern may have for our understanding of his fiction.

An astronomer, physicist, mathematician, and philosopher, among other things, Peirce presents a complex case for study. But his interest in the nature of human knowledge and his development of a science of signs to account for that knowledge are apparently what most attracted Percy's interest. Today Peirce is primarily remembered as the founder of pragmatic philosophy—or pragmaticism as he preferred to call it—but this doctrine was only one element in a much larger metaphysic. To fully delineate the complex principles of pragmatism, for instance, Peirce felt he first needed to investigate the function of logic. After all, he reasoned, if pragmatic knowledge depends on man's *ideas* of the effects which things have, then a right understanding of the manner in which those ideas are formulated was a necessity. He theorized that man's actions mirror an all-embracing animistic principle of cosmic love which infuses its character into all things. According to his "agapastic" doctrine, "nature fecundates the mind of man with ideas which, when those ideas grow up, will resemble their father, Nature."[2] All such ideas, though, are couched in terms of signs, so that, Peirce believed, "every thought is a sign" and "we have no power of thinking without signs."[3] As part of a thorough investigation into the nature and function of knowledge, then, Peirce was naturally led to analyze the types and functions of signs, thereby pioneering the modern study of semiotics.

What the present-day semiotic and structuralist movements have taken from Peirce, though, is not this unified vision but his rigorous and systematic approach to signs, his transformation of sign analysis into a science. Peirce defined a sign as "something which stands to somebody for something in some respect or capacity. It addresses somebody, that is, creates in the mind of that person an equivalent sign, or perhaps a more developed sign" (*PW*, p. 99). According to the nature of the sign, he then delineated three general categories of signs; and by combining these types, Peirce found that he could distinguish ten large classes of sign activity and 66 subclasses.[4] Through this complex schematization, Peirce asserted two essential semiotic propositions: 1) "anything which can be isolated, then connected with something else and 'interpreted,' can function as a sign"; and 2) such categories finally make possible "the analysis of the process of 'knowing' itself," of understanding "how knowledge is possible."[5]

Both of these propositions seem to focus exclusively on the real or implied relation between the sign and its object, or as de Saussure described it, between the signifier and the signified. Such a view apparently reduces human knowledge to a binary system or a series of paired opposites. It accords well with behavioral theory which suggests that language represents little more than a stimulus-response event occurring between two organisms, a theory that Percy comes to reject as being a reductive view of the human side of signification. For Percy language is the uniquely human form of sign usage, involving much more than any cause-effect relationship. The behavioral view, he suggests, overlooks this uniqueness by failing to account for the "coupling" activity which language involves, that *meaning* relation asserted between every word and referent: "to set forth language as a sequence of stimuli and responses overlooks the salient trait of symbolic behavior: Symbols, words, not only call forth responses; they also denote things, name things for . . . speakers."[6] Because of this reductiveness, a binary language theory also tends to diminish man to the level of another reactive organism, not markedly different from an animal responding to its environmental stimuli or a machine which clicks off/on, yes/no according to whatever data it receives.

Of course, language and sign usage are not necessarily synonymous, and many of Percy's objections apply only when one considers language as simply one more element in the large category of semiotic. Actually, Peirce had sharply distinguished between automatic and meaningful relations, but, as Percy explains, perhaps because his semiotic was "part and parcel of a heavy metaphysic and so could hardly be seen as something that happened among persons, words, and things" (*MB*, p. 39), it has often been misrepresented. Robert Coles in his recent study of Percy suggests that Peirce's work "straddles delicately the world of faith and the world of precise scientific observation";[7] and this is a conjunction which most linguists, for obvious reasons, find difficult to accept. At the same time, though, it is a combination in keeping with Percy's holistic approach to the problems of human nature and language use. A closer look at Peirce's three general categories of signs will show this full effect which his work has had on Percy's own linguistic discriminations.

Two of Peirce's three classes have little bearing on Percy's work, since neither specifically addresses the question of human language. These distinctions are those according to "kind, that is, by the sorts of entities that can do the work of a sign," and also "according to the nature of the objects they signify."[8] Of more importance for proper linguistic study is Peirce's classification in terms of "the relation of significance" between a sign and its object, that is, "the respect or capacity in which the sign stands for its object." Peirce did not suggest only a single type of relationship, as that behavioral perspective might lead us to believe, but three distinct kinds of sign—icon, index, and symbol, the latter of which embraces the human language act as Percy interprets it.

According to Peirce, these signs could be classified as either "genuine" or "degenerate," depending on the nature of the relation between the sign and its object, and specifically whether or not the sign involves a truly "triadic" relationship. By the term triadic he meant an "action, or influence, which is, or involves, a cooperation of *three* subjects, such as a sign, its object, and its interpretant, this tri-relative influence not being in any way resolvable into actions between pairs" (*PW*, p. 282). The significance of this three-cornered relationship is that it accounts for the involvement of the human intellect and thus for the *meaning* which man derives from his use of symbols. As Peirce explained, "Every physical force reacts between a pair of particles, either of which may serve as an index of the other. On the other hand, we shall find that every intellectual operation involves a triad" (*PW*, p. 114). Consequently, while the "dynamical, or dyadic" may serve as a sufficient model for *automatic* associations, for reactions involving a sign and an object, any correspondence containing an assertion of *meaning* will be "inexpressible by means of dyadic relations," since meaning could derive solely from "intelligent, or triadic action" (*PW*, p. 274), from that mysterious operation of the human intellect whereby one draws relations between elements of his world.

A degenerate sign, therefore, is basically binary in form; as John Fitzgerald explains it, "the foundation for the relation between the sign and its object is independent of a knower."[9] It is on this level that both the icon and the index function. The former is "a sign which refers to the Object that it denotes merely by virtue of characters of its own" (*PW*, p. 102); it implies a simple resemblance of qualities between the sign and some other entity and may be only an "accidental" relationship. The latter involves a stimulus-response type of relation in which the index is "physically connected with its object; they make an organic pair, but the interpreting mind has nothing to do with this connection, except remarking it, after it is established." A genuine sign, on the other hand, cannot be reduced to a binary model, for it *includes the notion of the interpreter, of the human mind, in its very structure*. Only the symbol fits the criteria of genuineness since it alone "is connected with its object by virtue of the idea of the symbol-using mind" (*PW*, p. 114). In keeping with the focus of a pragmatic philosophy, Peirce placed the burden of meaning—of genuineness—not on external objects or actions, but on man himself as he interacts with those externals.

In the opening of *The Message in the Bottle* Percy hints at his basic sympathy with such a focus. His work, he declares, "is about two things, man's strange behavior and man's strange gift of language, and about how understanding the latter might help in understanding the former" (*MB*, p. 9). What this statement of purpose suggests is that Percy is paramountly concerned with modern man's "strange behavior," particularly his sense of alienation, and that the main function of his linguistic theories is to shed some light on that human condition. He found that he might best accomplish this through an adaptation of those polarities of dyadic/triadic, degenerate/genuine which Peirce had proposed.

Fortunately Percy has eliminated much of the esoteric terminology for which Peirce is rather infamous. Simplifying his predecessor's distinctions, Percy focuses on the difference between a sign and a symbol. The former he defines as "an element in the environment which, through congenital or acquired patterns of behavior, directs the organism to something else, this something else being understood either as some other element or simply as biologically relevant behavior" (*MB*, p. 199). With this definition Percy is able to account for the behavioral view of human language as nothing more than a stimulus-response action. He thus defines a symbol in contrast as an element "qualitatively different from sign behavior"; it "does not direct our attention to something else, as a sign does. It does not direct at all. It 'means' something else. It somehow comes to contain within itself the thing it means" (*MB*, p. 153). This is the realm of most human communication and certainly of all that bears *meaning*. While the sign is dyadic and effect-oriented, involving a causal relation between itself and some object, the symbol is triadic and meaningful, operating through that interrelationship of itself, an interpretant, and an object—just as Peirce had first outlined.

What this triad offered Percy was a way of reinstating the basic human element to its rightful place in any consideration of the workings of language. Behavioral theory, he found, seems to downplay "those very features of language behavior which set it apart from other forms of animal communication," essentially suggesting that "human language must not be different in kind from communication in other species" (*MB*, pp. 303, 300). One major problem with such an approach is that it fails to account for the language user, man himself, and in support Percy cites Margaret Mead's belief that even "an ideally refined behaviorism could explain the behavior of the observed subject but not that of the observing behaviorist" (*MB*, p. 190). With Peirce's triad, though, the mind of the language user becomes a crucial element of the explanation, for "if there were no interpretant" there could effectively be no symbolic event (*PW*, p. 104). Armed with this trinary model, Percy found that he could properly begin to study man through an analysis of his language activity.

As a first step Percy attempts to outline precisely what the relationship between man and his linguistic activity is. He suggests that there is a "universal symbolic function of the human mind" which results in a "basic human need of symbolization" (*MB*, pp. 292, 296). This "need to know" through the use of symbols is one of the most fundamental human characteristics and an urge so strong that its denial may precipitate an acute "disability" which "can range from a simple insentience . . . to acute anxiety before a pressing something which is unformulated" (*MB*, p. 281). To fulfill his most basic needs, then, man must carry out his symbolizing role; as Percy puts it, "I cannot know anything at all unless I symbolize it" (*MB*, p. 72).

A major problem afflicting modern man, Percy speculates, is that he too often fails to enact this "uniquely human" role; that is, many people seem to speak as if language were simply a polite noise they had to make in order to elicit a response from a companion, or—worse yet—they fail to speak at all, lapsing into "a cocoon of dead silence"

(*MB*, p. 22). In great part this problem arises from the way we approach others through language. Peirce's emphasis was on the individual human mind, but as Percy notes, symbolization can never involve only one person: "Every symbolic formulation . . . requires a real or posited *someone else* for whom the symbol is intended as meaningful" (*MB*, p. 271). To avoid shortchanging the function of language as a communication *between* people, as an intersubjective act, Percy thus evolved another, more inclusive schema to complement Peirce's original triad.

Peirce did make a few, tentative references to that "circle of society" within which symbolism occurs (*PW*, p. 258), and apparently the notion of community underlay his conception of language usage. One of his interpreters, James Feibleman, has described this intersubjective emphasis in Peirce's philosophy: "communication is made possible by a universe held in common through experience."[10] For Percy this intersubjective element becomes explicit, forming an integral part of his language model. Percy seems to echo Peirce when he asserts, "The *I think* is only made possible by a prior mutuality: *we name*" (*MB*, p. 275). In Percy's view, therefore, man never speaks in a vacuum, never "names" solely for himself; rather, a real or implied community is intended by every use of language: "By the very nature of symbolic meaning, there must be *two* 'organisms' in the meaning relation, one who gives the name and one for whom the name becomes meaningful. The very essence of symbolization is an entering into a *mutuality* toward that which is symbolized" (*MB*, p. 256). Percy goes so far as to suggest that without this communal situation, in a world where symbols were not "held in common" by people, language would be impossible: "It is inconceivable that a human being raised apart from other humans should ever discover symbolization" (*MB*, p. 270). Man, then, is a communal creature, and his language, properly conceived of, must account for this fact. Consequently, to the Peircean triad of symbol, interpretant, and object, Percy adds another triangular relationship, one which describes symbolization's natural "*triad of existents: I, the object, you*" (*MB*, p. 281). The two triangular patterns are congruent and thus form a coherent existential description of the human language act:

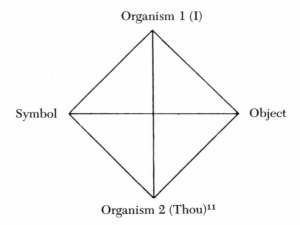

Organism 1 (I)

Symbol   Object

Organism 2 (Thou)[11]

According to Percy, therefore, we cannot be content with describing language simply as a collection of noun phrases, verb phrases, and functors which act according to stimulus-response models. Nor should we think of it in Chomsky's terms, as purely a correlation of deep structures and surface structures governed by a set of transformational rules. Drawing primarily on the work of Peirce, he holds that language is first and foremost a communication involving a denotative act and a coupling principle. Man *names* something, thereby asserting a vital connection between the symbol and its object. Moreover, he names for others; that is, just as he couples word and object, so too does he forge a bond—a linguistic one—between himself and the other inhabitants of his world through this most fundamental human action. Both of these coupling principles are needed to accurately depict what occurs when men use that one unique faculty "which even Darwin agreed sets them apart from the beasts" (*MB*, p. 16).

Once brought into this focus, a linguistic study may yield interesting implications for the study of man. Take for an example the situation of the modern, alienated man—as Percy does in each of his novels. Such a figure feels singularly estranged from others and what they hold meaningful; he observes that community of which he is a part to be slowly disintegrating. Coincident with this sense of alienation and disintegration, Percy notes, often comes a failure of human communication. People no longer talk, and when they do, it is often in almost meaningless clichés or, in what is equally meaningless to many, an elitist or technical jargon. Either silence or triteness thus seems to be the alternatives this modern man faces. Consequently, he either fails to speak at all to his fellow men or he liberally lards his conversation with cant phrases like "love, truth, peace, freedom, and the sacredness of the individual, since, for one thing, these prescriptions are open to almost any reading" (MB, p. 19), and hence are practically meaningless.[12]

As a Catholic writer following in the tradition of Kierkegaard and Gabriel Marcel, Percy believes that this alienation is partly the natural consequence of that primal Fall of Man, that universal estrangement from God and the meaning which He infused into the world. But in addition to this "historical" predicament, Percy notes what he thinks is a much more recent phenomenon, a striking correlation between this gradual loss of meaning in our everyday communications and the increasingly alienated feeling of modern man. Perhaps man has finally come to the point, Percy suggests, where he no longer adequately uses or even properly understands that gift of language by which he deals with his fallen world. A converse and more hopeful principle also suggests itself; if man recognizes this interrelationship, he may uncover a way of coping with his situation through those linguistic abilities.

Through his linguistic model, Percy holds out the hope that proper communication can help reverse this modern tendency and better enable man to deal with his natural condition as "exile and wanderer" (MB, p. 111). According to that first or Peircean triad, a symbol enables man to "know" his world; it thereby functions existentially, allowing him to affirm his own existence or position in the world as the "knower" of his domain. Secondly, both triads suggest what might be termed a negentropic function for language; that is, they imply that language brings meaning into the world anew and so helps to restore order and forestall those chaotic forces which seem to abound in modern times. In short, the information which true communication can bring may counter the ongoing disintegrative action of entropy.[13] Third, Percy's second triad indicates that language, by its very nature, involves and strengthens human intersubjectivity. Through language man becomes truly related to other men, a vital part of a community of fellow knowers, all functioning communally to restore meaning and hence order into their world. Hopefully, such an infusion of human understanding and compassion might enable us to experience a re-nascence of "love, truth, peace, freedom"; and reciprocally, some of those cant phrases we so often speak might finally begin to take on real meaning.

What we might ask at this point is just how far Percy has taken this triad borrowed from Peirce. Does it represent a philosophic-religious-linguistic interest totally separate from his novelist voca-tion?[14] Or does his fiction also mirror these multiple concerns, and especially this triadic approach to the human situation? He seems to have partially answered our question in *Message in the Bottle* where he describes the proper function of the modern novelist. As he sees it, "the novelist deals first and last with individuals," particularly those who have "very nearly come to the end of the line" (*MB*, pp. 108, 112). This predicament stems from the failure of a "radical bond . . . which connects man with reality" (*MB*, p. 102), and it is the novelist's task to call man's attention to this breakdown; "in his confused Orphic way," he tries "to tell us something we would do well to listen to" (*MB*, p. 107). By communicating this vision, he may restore that vital bond, coupling man to his world and conferring meaning where even the hope for something meaningful has been forgotten. In sum, the novelist initiates a triad with himself as speaker to a listening public, and he functions through the symbolic value of his novel—a symbol writ large—which serves his public as a very vital "message in the bottle."

Whether this linguistic pattern infuses Percy's novels themselves is another matter. Complicating the issue is the fact that in almost the same breath Percy has denied any connection between his language theory and his fiction, yet he has practically outlined just such an interdependence. While working on *Lancelot*, for example, he freely described the triadic situation he wished to create:

a man finds himself in some sort of a cell—it's not clear whether it's a prison cell or a sanitorium cell. He's there for several reasons—he's not quite sure, as a matter of fact he's amnesic. But he's very much aware that the language is worn out. And in the next room there's a woman who's in a state of catatonia; she's also mute, she's retreated from language. So he conceives the idea of trying to communicate with her by knocking on the wall. . . . what I had in mind was the wearing out of language and the creation of new language. . . . They're in adjoining cells, and their windows let on to the same scene, which is a very narrow slice of New Orleans, uptown New Orleans. It's a corner of the old Lafayette Cemetery, and a slice of the levee, and a slice of a movie theatre—but you can see a lot, you know. It's a triad. . . . So this man is in this cell and he likes it there, because it's the purest kind of triadic situation—and "I" and a "thou," something to look at and an opportunity to create a language, like Adam and Eve.[15]

The prison cells symbolize that distancing of self from the world and others which Percy sees as a characteristic of modern man's alienation. As this man and woman demonstrate, though, language can counter this predicament, particularly as it mediates between people to form that fundamental intersubjective relation of speaker and listener. The larger structure of *Lancelot* also bears the stamp of this triadic pattern, as it consists of a dialogue-communication between the alienated title-character and Percival, a priest and former friend, in which we move from a confession of mass murder to an affirmation of life and community. Their conversation—and the novel as well—ends with a single, resounding *"Yes"* from Percival, an affirmation clearly in keeping with the potential that Percy's language model promises.

While Percy has not outlined such a triadic strategy for his other novels, similar linguistic predicaments play significant roles in each of them. In *The Moviegoer*, for instance, Binx Bolling's confrontations with his Aunt Emily attest to the fact that language has become "worn out"; as Emily notes, they can no longer communicate because their words no longer "mean roughly the same thing" (*M*, p. 222). In *Love in the Ruins* silence is a common characteristic. After Tom More's early discovery of More's Syndrome, "there followed twenty years of silence and decline" (*LR*, p. 24), and Tom's friend Mr. Ives is about to be committed to the Happy Isles Separation Center for stubbornly refusing to speak to the behaviorists in control. *The Last Gentleman* provides even more obvious parallels, for Will Barrett, like Lancelot, has been in an asylum where he met a girl who "had not spoken to anyone for two years—she had not uttered a single word." Just by recollecting her name and talking to her, though—" 'Aren't you Margaret Rich?' " he asks—Will brings her out of that silence (he en*rich*es her) and she begins to speak again (*LG*, pp. 56–57). Likewise, Val infuses new life into the Tyree children who were "brought up in silence." She teaches them to "name" things—a "pencil or hawk or wallet"—and notes that "when they do suddenly break into the world of language, it is something to see. They are like Adam on the First Day" (*LG*, pp. 299, 301).

Perhaps more obvious is the fact that all of Percy's stories center around an isolated modern man, alienated from a proper knowledge of or relation to his world and fellow man, and seeking a restoration of that vital connection. His heroes begin in isolation but move to an intersubjective relationship by activating their communicative powers; specifically, each effects a triadic union by involving himself with another person through a very literal "naming" act. Binx Bolling, for example, finally opts for human commitment over his previous merry-go-round of pointless love affairs when, in conversation with another possible "conquest," he suddenly awakens to his situation and *names* Kate as his fiancée. Will Barrett offers his own name to Sutter Vaught—"I, Will Barrett, . . . need you and want you to come back" (*LG*, p. 409)—as a pledge of his sincerity and care; as a result, he saves Sutter's life and perhaps injects some new meaning into his own. In *Love in the Ruins* Tom More calls upon his *name*sake, "*Sir Thomas More, kinsman, saint, best dearest merriest of Englishmen*" (*LR*, p. 376), to save him and his nurse Ellen. The success of this naming is attested to by the close of the novel which finds Tom and Ellen, his new wife, in bed, united in anticipation of Christmas morning and a hopeful spiritual renascence for their community. In each case, a naming act completes a triadic bond and thereby engenders a new human situation, what almost seems an Edenic one. "Like Adam and Eve," these people are ready to begin the fundamental human task of inhabiting and knowing their world. It is, to be sure, still a fallen world, but then that may be precisely why we have language anyway; as Percy offers, "we do know, not as the angels know and not as dogs know but as men, who must know one thing through the mirror of another" (*MB*, p. 82).

Despite this evidence, Percy has denied any connection between his linguistic triads and his fiction. In fact, he has flatly stated that his "interest in language theory" and his "practice as a novelist" have "very little to do with each other. Maybe it's just as well. God help us if a novelist was thinking in terms of theoretical linguistics when he was writing. It'd be pretty bad."[16] Of course, according to *Message in the*

Bottle we should be in even greater need of God's help if we did not awake to the creative capacity inherent in our language. In all of his writings Percy speaks fluently and powerfully to modern man about his predicament, and in so speaking perhaps he cannot avoid following his own outline for meaningful communication. A kind of reciprocal relationship may therefore hold here, with the success of Percy's fiction serving as best evidence of the validity of his linguistic proposals.

When viewed in this light, Percy's fiction also seems to fit more into the mainstream of contemporary American literature which similarly places language in just such a crucial role. Indeed, in the work of writers like John Barth, Ronald Sukenick, and Donald Barthelme it frequently becomes, after a manner, the basic subject matter of the fiction, as they continually fashion narratives *about* narrative, stories concerned with the writing of stories. The fundamental goal of this self-reflexive approach is to place the act of writing, of communicating through words, into a new perspective. When these most basic elements of narrative become a central plot concern, a newly whole and organic fiction emerges, one calling attention to the essential limitations of the fictional process in hope that an acknowledgment of these limitations will, in some degree, free the fiction from them. After all, fiction by its very nature involves a paradox—it is a lie-telling to probe at the truth of life; and perhaps the ultimate lie involved in the fictional process is that convention of realism, the belief that those words grant us an access to life just as it is, offering an immediate, truthful, and reliable representation of reality. Calling attention to the act of writing the fiction, however, shatters this "reality illusion" while asserting a new and at least minimally truthful premise from which the fiction might start afresh. A reflexive fiction, then, admits the lie, confesses its own limitations—its *human*ness, if you will—but by so doing it offers a basic truth from which one can approach and evaluate the life it depicts. The hope is that the creation of this fundamental level of certitude will open the possibility for growth, that one truth will, in turn, engender others and so provide some value for man.

Percy never actually foregrounds his fiction the way a Barth or Sukenick might; that is, at no time does the act of writing or using words to tell a story ever become the major concern of his narratives. Yet his novels evidence every bit as much regard for the creative powers of language. While working from a similar impulse, Percy foregrounds not the act of telling a story, as do his contemporaries, but an act even prior to that and one in which all storytelling is rooted— the basic act of naming or symbolization. The vital importance of this naming process is Percy's fundamental truth, that upon which he grounds all of his fictional constructs. It constitutes that act whereby man brings into being both world and self, and so generates the possibility for further growth, for a continuation of the life process.

Against this background, that interweaving of linguistic and fictional concerns hardly seems wrong; in fact, the absence of such a unity of interests should have been much more curious. In Percy's case it has definitely not resulted in any "bad" fiction, or else the majority of critics have been badly mistaken. Throughout his canon Percy displays this unity of concerns and a unity of vision, and it is precisely this oneness, I would argue, that makes his work so intriguing yet accessible. In both his linguistic and fictional endeavors, Percy has attempted to sketch out exactly what plagues modern man and to offer a possible counter to this problem. As he has pointed out, this is "an age when communication theory and technique reached its peak" (*MB*, p. 25), but when most men have found themselves with nothing to say to their fellow men, and when even many artists only reiterate the despairing message that there is "nothing to be done." The task for the artist, as for the ordinary man, however, is to speak into this human silence and thereby draw man back into a world of meaningful relations. To this end, Percy has rummaged about in his philosophical heritage, resurrected a long-neglected approach to language, and applied it in a holistic fashion to the modern human situation. Beginning with Peirce's linguistic triad, Percy has attempted not only to explain *how* man communicates, but also to help him better carry out this most vital of human tasks.

NOTES

[1]I do not wish to suggest that Peirce has been the sole influence on the development of Percy's linguistic views. To be sure, one can find repeated references to Susanne Langer, Ernst Cassirer, Edward Sapir, and Noam Chomsky, among others, throughout Percy's writings; as Lewis Lawson notes, "Percy cannot be accused of leapfrogging the research in the field to proclaim his revelation—he is much too dedicated to science for that maneuver," "Walker Percy as Martian Visitor," *The Southern Literary Journal*, 8 (Spring 1976), 111. Peirce, however, seems to be the one figure who most fully embodies Percy's own linguistic thinking and certainly the one to whom he most frequently refers.

[2]*Essays in the Philosophy of Science*, ed. Vincent Thomas (Indianapolis: Bobbs-Merrill Co., 1957), p. 238.

[3]*Philosophical Writings of Peirce*, ed. Justus Buchler (New York: Dover, 1955), p. 230. Subsequent references are in the text as *PW*.

[4]See also C. M. Smith's essay, "The Aesthetics of Charles Sanders Peirce," in *The Journal of Aesthetics and Art Criticism*, 31 (Fall 1972), 21–29, for a detailed discussion of Peirce's sign classifications.

[5]I am indebted here to Terence Hawkes's discussion of Peirce and semiotics in *Structuralism and Semiotics* (Berkeley: Univ. of California Press, 1977), p. 128.

[6]*The Message in the Bottle* (New York: Noonday, 1975), p. 194. All references to Percy's works are cited in the text.

[7]*Walker Percy: An American Search* (Boston: Little, Brown and Co., 1978), p. 70.

[8]Smith, pp. 23, 24.

[9]*Peirce's Theory of Signs as Foundation for Pragmatism* (The Hague: Mouton, 1966), p. 45.

[10]*An Introduction to Peirce's Philosophy* (New York: Harper & Brothers, 1946), p. 199.

[11]In *Message in the Bottle* Percy alternately describes the naming act as a pair of triadic relations and as a single "tetradic" or four-cornered relation consisting of symbol, object, speaker (an "I"), and listener (a "Thou"). These are not mutually exclusive or contradictory models though, but, as the explanatory diagram indicates, simply alternative ways of viewing the same linguistic fact (see pp. 200, 299).

[12]In his essay "Mississippi: The Fallen Paradise," *Harper's*, 230 (1965), 166–72, Percy notes that this tendency is particularly marked in the modern South, probably because Southerners have for so long prided themselves on their maintenance of these traditional values and thus have kept up a degree of confidence in the terminology associated with them. In this context we might also note the Charles Manson type of murderer in *Love in the Ruins* who nevertheless "believes in love, the environment, and freedom of the individual."

[13]See also my discussion of entropy and communication in an earlier essay, "Walker Percy's Language of Creation," *The Southern Quarterly*, 16 (1978), 115–16.

[14]Lewis Lawson suggests that Percy would "turn to fiction whenever he became stymied in his study" of language (p. 107). This conclusion is in keeping with Percy's own account, but it downplays the complex interrelationships of Percy's multiple concerns.

[15]"Talking about Talking: An Interview with Walker Percy," *New Orleans Review*, 5 (1976), 17.

[16]"Talking about Talking," p. 16.

Percy's Bludgeon:
Message and Narrative Strategy

ROBERT H. BRINKMEYER, JR.

To be an American Christian novelist nowadays is no simple vocation, as Walker Percy knows. The Christian novelist's dilemma, writes Percy in "Notes for a Novel about the End of the World," is that "though he professes a belief which he holds saves himself and the world and nourishes his art besides, it is also true that Christianity seems in some sense to have failed. Its vocabulary is worn out. This twin failure raises problems for a man who is a Christian and whose trade is with words." The novelist of faith finds himself in an extremely precarious position, addressing readers who, by and large, find his vision of things outmoded and his vocabulary meaningless. "The old words of grace," Percy continues, "are worn smooth as poker chips and a certain devaluation has occurred, like a poker chip after it is cashed in" (*MB*, p. 116). What paths, then, do lie open to a Christian writer?

One way to get around these obstacles would be simply to ignore them. Some Christian novelists do manage to take no account of the skepticism and secularism of so many modern readers. Henry Morton Robinson's *The Cardinal* is an example. But this is the easy way out, an evasion of the issues, for novelists like Robinson do not mirror in their art the world about them, nor do they create a vital bond of communication between reader and writer.

But another, more strenuous course is to follow the lead of Flannery O'Connor. This Catholic writer works by continually assaulting her readers' rational sensibilities to prepare them for the larger Christian vision that permeates her work. Percy says, "In answer to a question about why she created such bizarre characters, she replied that for the

80

near-blind you have to draw very large, simple caricatures" (*MB*, p. 118).

The Christian writer, says Percy, cannot afford to ignore his audience's shortcomings. Indeed, he must write with these deficiencies specifically in mind; he must employ fictional techniques of shock and insult to reveal to his readers the gaps in their understanding of the world. The great hope harbored by a Christian writer, according to Percy, is that his readers, contemplating the eternal questions of identity and fate and the chaotic nature of life, will begin to look beyond the walls of their own heads.

To understand how Percy's ideas on the role of the Christian novelist affect his own fiction—what he specifically tries to accomplish in his own work—one must first understand how he views this age and the audience to whom he writes. Percy feels the general orientation of the modern age is basically scientific, theorizing that "man is an organism among other organisms" (*MB*, p. 19). According to this view, since man is only an organism in an environment, he should be able to achieve perfect happiness as he adapts his environment to fit his physical needs. This way of thinking rejects those depressing old ideas about the Fall which claimed that the state of alienation was a result of man's having separated himself from God. With the tremendous powers of scientific technology and humanistic education, most of us implicitly believe, the human race can look forward to living happily ever after.

But, says Percy, the modern view is no longer tenable because what should have happened hasn't. What he means by all this becomes specifically, unarguably obvious from the questions opening "The Delta Factor":

> Why does man feel so sad in the twentieth century?
> Why does man feel so bad in the very age when, more than in any other age, he has succeeded in satisfying his needs and making over the world for his own use?
> Why has man entered on an orgy of war, murder, torture, and self-destruction unparalleled in history and in the very century when he had hoped to see the dawn of universal peace and brotherhood?
> Why do people often feel bad in good environments and good in bad environments? (*MB*, p. 3)

The theories of the scientists and humanists are founded on an idea of man as a powerful organism in a pliant environment; they leave no room to account for these symptoms of profound weakness and discontent.

Because the modern view of man as organism no longer works, and because the Judeo-Christian conception of man as something more than an organism—he has a soul—is disregarded, people today have no system of belief to use in understanding their lives. There are of course many who place no importance on such matters, or who in Percy's words from "The Delta Factor," "are quite content to live out their lives as the organisms and consumer units their scientists understand them to be" (*MB*, p. 19). They can often live fairly placid—and meaningless—lives. But others must daily endure bewildering pain and fear, without having the means to understand or transcend.

For Percy this experience of fear and discontent is precisely the human condition. As a Catholic, he believes that man is in actual fact a castaway, cut off from God, homeless (even in the bosom of his family)—not because he is psychologically sick, but very simply because since Adam we have all lost our rightful home. And as Percy writes in "The Message in the Bottle," true despair is not the knowledge that one's life is out of joint but the pretence that all is well: "The worst of all despairs is to imagine one at home when one is really homeless" (*MB*, p. 144).

Two types of readers then might pick up a Walker Percy book: an alienated reader who knows he is alienated and an alienated reader who imagines that he is not. Remembering that Percy feels keenly that he must write with his audience's attitudes and sensitivities in mind, I want to suggest here how Percy's perceptions of his audience have affected the composition of his novels.

Percy's first two novels, *The Moviegoer* and *The Last Gentleman*, seem to me to have been written with readers in mind who already feel their alienation from their own deeper selves and from the center of life. In "The Man on the Train," Percy describes a narrative strategy, the one I believe he uses in these two books to reach his readers. Here he tells what happens when an alienated commuter reads a book about another alienated commuter: ". . . the reading commuter re-joices in the speakability of his alienation and in the triple alliance of himself, the alienated character, and the author. His mood is affirma-tory and glad: Yes! that is how it is!—which is an aesthetic reversal of alienation" (*MB*, p. 83). Besides allowing the reader to join in an alliance with the character and author, the novels also point the way out for those who are alienated and don't know why, as both end with alienated heroes reaching a religious perception of their own positions in the world. Percy's other readers, ostensibly contented with their lives, presumably find no disturbing message in these two novels. They might well enjoy on a superficial level the adventures of Percy's heroes, and even understand Percy's criticism of their life-style, but there is no reason why they should be terribly moved by the novels. Neither work shockingly indicts modern life, except for the comments in Sutter's notebook in *The Last Gentleman*; but the criti-cism there is far from being in the forefront of the novel, and much of its effect is lost in its tough style. No violent assaults take place on the contented reader's rational sensibilities which could, after the fashion of Flannery O'Connor's fiction, shock him from his locked-in world of "everydayness."

With Percy's third and fourth novels, *Love in the Ruins* and *Lan-celot*, Percy, I think, shifts his attention from the consciously alienated readers to the larger audience of the placid and self-satisfied. *Love in the Ruins* is in many ways very similar to his previous novels. For instance, another "bad Catholic," adrift in his world, finally reaches a religious awareness of the human condition. But this novel em-phasizes what Percy calls the "everyday tools of the trade" of the Christian novelist—"violence, shock, comedy, insult, the bizarre." And the novel has a pressing, urgent tone; we're closer to the end than you think, he seems to be saying. His primary fictional strategy now is to shock the complacent reader, jolt him by putting him through an ordeal and impel him to look more critically at his world of "every-dayness." He may see that he, like all human beings since the Fall, is essentially a castaway, a sojourner passing through this life to an eternal home. In "Notes for a Novel about the End of the World," Percy writes about *Love in the Ruins*: "Perhaps it is only through the conjuring up of catastrophe, the destruction of all Exxon signs, and the sprouting of vines in the church pews, that the novelist can make vicarious use of catastrophe in order that he and his reader may come to themselves" (*MB*, p. 118).

Having a person come to himself, or see the true nature of himself and of the world, is an important idea in Percy's novels and essays. In the novels characters emerge from ordeals with their eyes burned clean, and in the essays one of Percy's favorite anecdotes is the story of the commuter who suffers a heart attack and regains consciousness with a new awareness of himself and of life. Having finished *Love in the Ruins* and having been jolted into an awareness of the knowledge of man's alienation from God, the reader is in a better position to accept what Percy in "The Message in the Bottle" calls "news from across the seas" (*MB*, p. 146)—the word of God brought by a priest or apostle, or through the sacrament of Christ's body and blood. For as Percy continues in this same essay, such news is "not news to a fallen man who is a castaway but believes himself to be at home in the world, for he does not recognize his own predicament. It is only news to a castaway who knows himself to be a castaway" (*MB*, p. 148). Percy does not pretend to be God's messenger—except in the sense that any person can be a vehicle of God's grace to another person. He does hope, however, to prepare the reader to listen when the messenger comes.

Lancelot is Percy's boldest attempt to jar the complacent reader and is certainly his most disturbing novel so far. While the novel is unmistakably his—with the hilarious songlike dialogue, the beautiful-absurd places and women, the quasiscientific precision of color and gesture and voice—here is a more intense and upsetting tone than he has used up till now. Violence and hatred for the first time take center stage. Percy has added some new weaponry to his assault on complacent readers.

During the opening pages of the novel, as we listen to Lancelot tell his story to Percival, his boyhood friend turned Roman Catholic priest, this new shift in strategy is not completely evident. There is a good deal of light-hearted humor, and Lancelot himself appears to be another of Percy's disoriented but attractive heroes. Percy, I believe, wants to lull the complacent reader into the book before he begins his therapeutic assault. Nobody likes to be on the wrong end of a satirical attack, and Percy wants the reader to be interested in the novel (simply so that he will read it) but also unprepared, with defenses down, when the tone shifts.

As the novel progresses, Lance's views of the world soon begin to lose their comic vitality, and we become aware that he himself is quite different from the wacked-out but gentle protagonists of Percy's other novels. Lance's observations soon become ravings. Time and again he blasts offensively worded indictments against society, focusing most scathingly on what he sees as the insidious forces of permissiveness, sexual and otherwise. Women, whose liberation infuriates Lance because his idol of the Southern belle falls before it, bear the brunt of his most caustic attacks (p. 177).

Lance's ideas and language are not easy to take, and most of the novel is anything but pleasant reading. But that is exactly what Percy intends. Lancelot's tirades are deliberately grotesque exaggerations designed to electrify the callous sensibilities of the complacent readers. This is a hazardous path for Percy to tread, for undoubtedly a lot of those readers will abandon the book in disgust. Percy hopes that for many others the violent insults and shocks of the novel will have a purgative effect, so that these readers will be propelled out of their locked-in confines of "everydayness." Once these readers begin to feel a little shook up, the novel speaks tellingly to them; for what *Lancelot* is ultimately about is the problem of what one does in today's madhouse society when one realizes its absurdity and one's fate of being a stranger in its midst.

Lancelot is the story of a man who, like the complacent readers at whom the novel is aimed, is locked into a stultifying routine. We watch what happens when he is shot into a new realm of freedom and action. His epiphany comes when he discovers he cannot be the father of his "daughter." As he steps free from the worn path of his old life, he finds himself at the entrance of a new world: "There was a sense of astonishment, of discovery, of a new world opening up, but the new world was totally unknown. Where does one go from here?" (p. 42). Lance's problem is also that of the suddenly uncomplacent reader of the novel. Consequently his actions take on a grand importance for the reader, for they represent one way to pass through this uncharted realm. The reader can learn from Lance's mistakes.

Lance declares that he will set out on a quest. " 'Evil,' " he says, "is surely the clue to this age, the only quest appropriate to the age. For everything and everyone's either wonderful or sick and nothing is evil" (p. 138), in the opinion of scientists and humanists. If he could find just one true sin, unmitigated and unexcused by today's limp amorality, then the old Judeo-Christian way of life would begin to make sense. Like Percy's other "bad Catholics," Lancelot might even return to the Church if his quest proves successful. Only the discovery of sin, he believes, could jolt him back into belief. Percy is using this same shock therapy on his readers. He smears their faces in the real ugliness of evil, hoping thereby to make them start looking around for its alternative.

Lance's first move, then, is an instinctive search for God, although he pursues this goal by way of a twisted and self-defeating plan. To discover sin, he hopes to see clearly and directly his wife's adultery by filming her in the act. Later he says the quest fails. He has not found sin, he claims, even though he actually walked in on his wife having sex with Jacoby (and wrestled with them, making their act even more real), committed adultery himself, and coldly calculated and executed a triple murder. To his disappointment, his act of murder brought him no sense of evil or guilt. All it came to, he says, was molecules and blood cells (p. 254). Society has reacted not by condemning him but by protecting and supporting him in a center for aberrant behavior.

After Lance becomes convinced that his quest revealed nothing, he plans his second action, that of rejecting both the present age and the Catholic faith, and building a new society, what he calls at one point "The New Reformation" (p. 156). He says that he could live in society as it is only if he could believe in God; but he cannot believe. What's more, Catholicism itself, Lance declares to Percival, has been diluted by modern permissiveness: "I might have tolerated you and your Catholic Church, and even joined it, if you had remained true to yourself. Now you're part of the age. You've the same fleas as the dogs you've lain down with" (p. 157). The old ways have nothing to offer him; Lance will start afresh, initiating a new order in that old womblike seat of Southern glory and defeat, the Shenandoah Valley.

Lance's new society will be based on the codes of courtesy and chivalry by which he believes noble men of the past acted. People will be self-reliant and will live simple, wholesome lives: "One will work and take care of one's own, live and let live, and behave with a decent respect toward others" (p. 158). Christian love is not part of the plan. As Cleanth Brooks points out, Lance is a thoroughgoing modern gnostic, confident his millenial vision will cure a corrupt world and certain that it is only through his own efforts that man can effect his salvation.[1] Put another way, Lance aspires to be one more of those prevalent figures in the American imagination, the New American Adam: he believes that by retreating to an unsettled piece of land (Virginia—the land of the virgin) he can begin anew, free from the taints of the past.

In some ways Lance's vision seems like *the* answer; compared to the chaos of modern civilization, a retreat to the woods to initiate a simpler life (such an American dream!) carries a good deal of appeal. But is Lance's plan the one which Percy wants his readers to endorse? Should we feel satisfied with Lance's vision of a new order? Does Lance possess the answer to modern alienation? No—and Percy gives us clues throughout the novel which point to the ultimate shortcomings of Lance's plan to heal man and society. There are also signposts leading the reader towards the other alternative, the only one which we can possibly suppose that Percy himself endorses. This is of course Christianity, represented here by the silent but patiently enduring priest Percival.

One way to understand the futility of Lance's dream is to compare it with the life Thomas More establishes at the end of *Love in the Ruins*. At first glance Lance's vision of a new way seems to coincide with More's new life: More has retreated with his new wife and family to an old brick slave cabin where they live a quiet life and enjoy the simple pleasures of good boots and hot morning grits. But upon closer examination, some crucial differences appear. Thomas More's rejection of modern emptiness and his achievement of inner peace include his acceptance—however reluctant—of Christian faith. More is not a new

Adam, starting anew without the taint of sin. Significantly, at the end of the book he attends confession for the first time in eleven years and feels ashamed of his sins. Lancelot's life, in contrast, will be one of purely secular chivalry, founded on anger not charity. When Percival hints at this shortcoming to his plan, Lance's reply is striking: "What did you whisper? Love? That I am full of hatred, anger? Don't talk to me of love until we shovel out the shit" (p. 179). Again in contrast to Thomas More, Lance believes he can cut himself off from the past and asserts that he is not responsible for the actions of his old life. But it is only a pipedream. Having refused the comfort of confession and absolution, Lance is bound forever to the numbness and emptiness which his sins have wrought in him. "I feel so cold, Percival," he says when he finishes his tale, and there is no possibility that running off to the Shenandoah Valley will cure his chill.

In contrast to Lance's ideas of a new order stands Percival's Catholicism. Although Percival is characterized throughout by his pensive silence (remember Percy has said that "the old words of grace are worn smooth as poker chips"), we are intended to understand that Percival's life is the alternative to Lance's. Particularly significant here is the fact that Percy offers only these two alternatives to the alienated reader searching for meaning. We can either follow the way of a murderer who sees himself as a new and innocent Adam, or we can go God's way. There is no middle ground.

Percy's strategy is simple: he forces the reader into a situation where he must choose between Lancelot and Percival, but only after he has revealed the ugliness at the heart of Lancelot's approach. The reader is compelled to listen to Percival, unless he is willing to consider himself an extremist burning with rage and described as appearing like "Lucifer blown out of hell" (p. 246). And Percy *points* the reader to Percival. In that final exchange, it is Percival who knows what he is doing, not Lancelot.

That Lancelot's vision ultimately comes up short next to Percival's should be no surprise when one remembers that Percy strikes corresponding chords between the action of the novel and the medieval legend of the quest for the Holy Grail. While there are several versions of the Grail legend (including Tennyson's *Idylls of the King* that Robert Coles discusses),[2] I think a more instructive comparison is

with the twelfth-century French *Queste del Saint Graal*. In this medieval tale, the Round Table society is beset from within by the sins of
various unchaste knights and ladies. To heal the kingdom King Arthur
sends his knights on the holiest quest possible, the search for the
chalice that Christ used at the Last Supper. Most of them fail, however, including the noble Lancelot, because their secular chivalry is
useless to bring them this highest, holiest privilege. Lancelot almost
succeeds, through his courage and great heart, but he is denied the
final victory because his highest allegiance is not to Christ but to the
chivalric ideals of love and honor. His best love is saved for Guine-
vere, not the Lord. Percival, on the other hand, is a true knight of
Christ and therefore is successful on his quest.

Both *Queste del Saint Graal* and *Lancelot* ultimately explore the
same crucial questions: can one initiate a new life, free from the
decadence of society, by practicing a purely secular chivalric code of
honor and simplicity? Or must one grapple with the significance of
Christ's love and death and resurrection? Both works end by affirming
the need to follow Christ.

"Very well. I've finished," says Lancelot at the end of *Lancelot*. "Is
there anything you wish to tell me before I leave?" (p. 257). "*Yes*"
answers Percival. This is the novel's last word. Lance's story and his
wild theorizing have come to an end. Now Percival has a chance to
follow behind him and point out to him the true path, just as Percy
hopes the jolted reader will someday listen to the voice of God's
messenger in his own life.

At the end of his essay "The Message in the Bottle," Percy talks
about what he hopes will happen to any once-complacent person who,
like the reader of *Lancelot*, has been shocked from his everydayness
and has become a castaway: "And what if the news the newsbearer
bears is the very news the castaway had been waiting for, news of
where he came from and who he is and what he must do, and what if
the newsbearer brought with him the means by which the castaway
may do what he must do? Well then, the castaway will, by the grace of
God, believe him" (*MB*, p. 149). Percy can bring his readers only so
far; that final step is up to them and God.

NOTES

[1]Cleanth Brooks, "Walker Percy and Modern Gnosticism," *The Southern Review*, 23 (Oct. 1977), 677–87.

[2]Robert Coles, *Walker Percy: An American Search* (Boston: Atlantic-Little, Brown, 1979), pp. 213–16.

Voices in the Wilderness:
The Prophets of O'Connor, Percy, and Powers

SUSAN S. KISSEL

With the publication of his fourth novel, *Lancelot*, Walker Percy's relationship to his fellow Catholic writers, Flannery O'Connor and J.F. Powers, should be much more obvious than before. There have always been important similarities among these three contemporary American literary artists—but the similarities have been overshadowed by the extreme differences in action, setting, character and style. Now it should be clear that what they have had to say about the modern Catholic Church and about contemporary American life has been, in fact, all the while, remarkably similar.

Lancelot Andrewes Lamar, the protagonist of Percy's latest novel, is, of course, a murderer—a man who has killed his wife and her lover and set fire to his historic Southern house, Belle Isle. One year later he confesses to his priest-psychiatrist-friend Percival:

> The truth is that during all the terrible events that night at Belle Isle, I felt nothing at all. Nothing good, nothing bad, not even a sense of discovery. I feel nothing now except a certain coldness.
> I feel so cold, Percival.
> Tell me the truth. Is everyone cold now or is it only I? (p. 253)

To read Lancelot's words is to remember the two protagonists of Flannery O'Connor's novels, heroes whom Josephine Hendin has called "so emotionally dead that they can perform the most outrageous acts without any conscious awareness or feelings of elation or despair."[1] Both Hazel Motes in *Wise Blood* and Tarwater in *The Violent Bear It Away* murder mechanically and deliberately to make things "right"—by erasing the forms of human life which repel them. In this way, too, Percy's Lancelot methodically sets out on his "quest for evil" (p. 138), determined to know and to obliterate the wickedness

91

and sinfulness of his own wife, her friends, and the modern world they represent. He murders not in a vindictive rage but, as he himself admits, coldly and ruthlessly—as do Hazel Motes and Tarwater, as well. Lancelot's brutal, destructive acts are the initial steps of his subsequent, grandiose plan "to start a new age. We shall start a new order of things . . . the Third Revolution" (pp. 156–57); he sets forth on this mission, assailing "the city of the dead" (p. 254), as have O'Connor's prophets, Hazel Motes and Tarwater, before him.

Lancelot is a man apart, a man without friends, an inmate of the New Orleans Center for Aberrant Behavior, as caught up in the "dark tunnel"[2] of himself as are O'Connor's obsessed prophets. But he has not always been that way; once Lancelot had been very active in college, "prominent on campus, debater, second-string all-S.E.C. halfback, Rhodes scholar, even 'smart,' that is, a sort of second-echelon Phi Beta Kappa" (p. 14); later he became a liberal lawyer, civil rights activist, Civil War historian, and master of the renovated Belle Isle tourist attraction—drifting slowly into idleness, purposelessness, and alcoholism before learning of his wife Margot's infidelity. Now, after the murder, he cultivates the isolated life, communicating with no one except his friend Percival and his fellow inmate, Anna, glorying in his little cell: "Have you noticed that the narrower the view the more you can see? For the first time I understand how old ladies can sit on their porches for years" (p. 3). When at the end of the novel he has been pronounced "psychiatrically fit and legally innocent" (p. 249), he presumably turns his back forever on the Sodom of modern America and sets forth to continue his solitary existence, this time in the rugged American past of the Shenandoah Valley.

In his final isolation from human society, Percy's Lancelot resembles not only the prophet-protagonists of O'Connor's two novels but also Father Urban, the transformed protagonist of J.F. Powers's *Morte D'Urban*—a sociable, outgoing priest who ultimately rejects the secular world of Great Plains, Minnesota and the clerical world of the Clementine Order over which he ironically presides at the end of the novel. Father Urban's withdrawal marks a complete reversal from his earlier "urban" gregariousness and spiritual ecumenicism, his philosophy that: "charity toward all, even when a few sharks get in among the swimmers, is always better than holier-than-thou singularity.

That, roughly speaking, was the mind of the Church."[3] At the end of *Morte D'Urban*, Father Urban, like Percy's one-time liberal lawyer Lancelot, has given up working in the world to promote social harmony and human justice; Father Urban's policy as Provincial is now to retreat into his office where he does "his best to see as few people as possible" (p. 308). Powers, too, compares his hero to "Sir Launcelot," that historic-mythic figure who "died to the world . . . [and] 'endure[d] such penance, in prayers, and fastings . . . [that] the noblest knight of the world . . . [in] abstinence . . . waxed full lean' " (p. 294).

"Dying to the world"—that is the central Christian experience which Percy's Lancelot, Powers's Father Urban, and O'Connor's prophets all undergo in the action of their respective novels. The world of social interrelationships, economic successes, and political achievements becomes, finally, irrelevant to each of these heroes. At the end of *Morte D'Urban* Father Urban refuses, as Father Provincial of his order, to become involved in the very Clementine struggles for power and for more effective public relations which had once engaged all of his attention; the narrator of "Dirge" comments on this change in Father Urban when he says: "Seldom had a new Provincial so badly disappointed the hopes and calculations of men. Many changes in personnel had been expected, but there had been few, and strangely, the men regarded as most likely to be affected, as almost certain to get the boot, were spared" (p. 306).

The prophet-protagonists of Flannery O'Connor's novels ultimately reject, as well, the wickedness of the world which had once lured them into renouncing Christ. In *Wise Blood* the blinded Hazel Motes "dies to the world," to the bewilderment of his landlady, Mrs. Flood: "She thought it would be a good thing if he had something to do with his hands, something to bring him out of himself and get him in connection with the real world again. She was certain he was out of connection with it; she was not certain at times that he even knew she existed" (p. 119). In the same way Tarwater in *The Violent Bear It Away* realizes, at last, that his "hunger . . . was the same as the old man's and that nothing on earth would fill him" (p. 446), that he is one "in a line of men whose lives were chosen to sustain [the hunger], who would wander in the world, strangers from that violent country where the silence is never broken except to shout the truth" (pp. 446–47).

Lancelot is the only one of Percy's protagonists who takes the final spiritual step of "dying to the world" in the manner of Father Urban, Hazel Motes, and Tarwater. The others, Binx Bolling, Will Barrett, and Dr. Thomas More, remain both in, and at a contemplative distance from, the modern world. Each finally rejects contemporary sexual morality to begin a monogamous relationship at the end of the novel; further, each plans to lead a simple, unpretentious life in the midst of a rapidly changing, often violent, tense and avaricious new South. Finally, although Will Barrett loses his special, acute perceptivity, Binx and Dr. Thomas More remain solitary observers who "watch and wait" (*LR*, p. 382) for that small clue which will clarify everything and give significance to human life. All of these Percy protagonists have taken definite spiritual postures in a society Percy exposes as having abandoned its soul, but Lancelot alone turns his back completely on the wickedness of the world to set forth a solitary prophet, a stranger wandering in an alien world, shouting the truth of modern society's sickness and corruption, determined to create a new world of honor and virtue and innocence.

The prophet-protagonists of these three contemporary Catholic writers "die to the world" in recognition of the evil of man and in deliberate decision to spend the rest of their lives in struggle against human wickedness. Thus, they differ radically from a society which believes that, as the Archbishop of Powers's "Prince of Darkness" explains: "today there are few saints, fewer sinners, and everybody is already saved. We are all heroes in search of an underdog. As for villains, the classic kind with no illusions about themselves, they are . . . extinct. The very devil, for instance—where the devil is the devil today, Father?"[4] Percy's Lancelot, too, stands apart from a world which sees itself as sinless, which believes that: "The mark of the age is that terrible things happen but there is no 'evil' involved. People are either crazy, miserable, or wonderful, so where does the 'evil' come in?" (p. 139) He searches determinedly for the Unholy Grail because, "If there is such a thing as sin, evil, a living malignant force, there must be a God!" (p. 52) In *Love in the Ruins*, Percy's protagonist, Dr. Thomas More, has met that "living malignant force" in the person of Art Immelmann, the "liaison" man between the public sector's Institute of Mental Health and the private sector's Ford, Carnegie, and Rockefeller foundations. Flannery O'Connor's Tarwater has also looked into the lavendar eyes of Satan himself in the final section of *The Violent Bear It Away*. The face of the devil has become so familiar, his behavior so pervasive, his voice so insistent, that these prophets find it essential, at last, to reject almost everything that has become everyday and commonplace in twentieth century American culture.

In the petty upsets of the rectory, the domestic conflicts of the backwoods Southern family, and the sexual, political, social upheavals of twentieth century urban American life, these three contemporary Catholic writers suggest the omnipresence of evil. At the beginning of *Lancelot* Percy defines his task as novelist in an epigraph from the *Purgatorio*:

> He sank so low that all means
>   for his salvation were gone,
>   except showing him the lost people.
> For this I visited the region of the dead . . .

Modern man, he feels, has lost his way and must, now, be led out of darkness; in the words of Powers's Archbishop of "Prince of Darkness," "We are now entering the whale's tail, Father. We must go back the way we came in" (p. 190). All three novelists point the way out of contemporary corruption and despair by having their protagonists "go back the way they came in." To do so their protagonists adopt outmoded, sometimes violent and bizarre, methods of struggling with evil, as this exchange between Hazel Motes and his landlady Mrs. Flood makes clear:

> "What's that wire around you for? It's not natural," she repeated.
> After a second he began to button the shirt. "It's natural," he said.
> "Well, it's not normal. It's like one of them gory stories, it's something that people have quit doing—like boiling in oil or being a saint or walling up cats," she said. "There's no reason for it. People have quit doing it."
> "They ain't quit doing it as long as I'm doing it," he said. (p. 122)

Hazel Motes blinds himself with lye, wraps his body in barbed wire, and puts gravel, glass, and pebbles in his shoes to exorcise the devil within and make himself "clean" (p. 122). He adopts the monastic life of abstinence and piety and, with Lancelot, Tarwater, and

Father Urban, retreats from the modern world, acting in "abnormal" ways, doing what other people have long ago "quit" doing, in order to punish himself for sin.

The Christianity manifest in these protagonists is an abrasive faith which refuses to accommodate itself either to modern society or to the modern Catholic Church. The prophets of O'Connor, Percy, and Powers offer their fellow man what Powers's Archbishop in "Prince of Darkness" offered the comfort-seeking Father Burner, "not peace but a sword" (p. 193)—words which occur again and again in Lancelot's "discussions" with Percival in Percy's latest novel. Lancelot attacks the Catholic Church, recalling its militant historical past, when he tells Percival: "I might have tolerated you and your Catholic Church, and even joined it, if you had remained true to yourself. Now you're part of the age. You've the same fleas as the dogs you've lain down with. I would have felt at home at Mont-Saint-Michel, the Mount of the Archangel with the flaming sword, or with Richard Coeur de Lion at Acre. They believed in a God who said he came not to bring peace but the sword." (p. 157). All three of these contemporary Catholic writers make clear through their fiction a belief that the modern Catholic Church must return to its more formidable, uncompromising, violent past. Lancelot laments, "There is only one way and we could have had it if you Catholics hadn't blown it: the old Catholic way. . . . Now you've . . . taken the sword from Christ" (pp. 176–77). The "Old Catholic way" is the way of "the stern Christ of the Sistine" (p. 178), the way of lonely, painful, religious martyrdom—the way of O'Connor's most touchingly human protagonist, the bewildered prophet O. E. Parker, weeping under the pecan tree, cast out of his house, with the "all-demanding eyes" of the "flat stern Byzantine Christ"[5] tattooed forever on his back. It is the way, too, of self-punishment and penance, of Dr. Thomas More of Percy's *Love in the Ruins* confessing his sins at last and donning the humbling sackcloth and ashes of the ancient Christian rite which Percy looks forward to having "John XXIV . . . revive [for] public penance, a practice of the early Church" (p. 399). The new prophet-figures of these three Catholic novelists all finally come to recognize the "all-demanding" nature of Christian faith, as foreign to modern Christianity as it is to everyday, contemporary life.

These prophet-heroes reject, too, the virtues of the modern religious ecumenical spirit: tolerance, forbearance, kindliness, patience, and love. Over and over, O'Connor's intellectual and liberal protagonists (Julian, Hulga, and Sheppard) must learn of their human fallibility, their moral weaknesses, and be punished for thinking so highly of themselves. As Hazel Motes tells his landlady Mrs. Flood, "if you believed in Jesus, you wouldn't be so good" (p. 120). Lancelot prophesies that "Christian love" will not be a part of the new age: "the new order will not be based on Catholicism or Communism or fascism or liberalism or capitalism or any ism at all, but simply on that stern rectitude valued by the new breed and marked by the violence which will attend its breach. We will not tolerate this age. Don't speak to me of Christian love. Whatever came of it? I'll tell you what came of it. It got mouthed off on the radio and TV from the pulpit and that was the end of it. The Jews knew better. Billy Graham lay down with Nixon and got up with a different set of fleas, but the Jewish prophets lived in deserts and wildernesses and had no part with corrupt kings" (p. 158).

This is the very lesson Father Urban in *Morte D'Urban* must learn, as well—that his charity towards corrupt individuals such as the wealthy Clementine patrons, Billy Cosgrove and Mrs. Thwaites, debases his impoverished Order rather than strengthens it, that it is not, as he had always believed, at all wise to "make friends . . . with the mammon of iniquity" (p. 21) in order to bring the Church into the lives of sinful men. As Monsignor Renton has advised Father Urban earlier in the novel, "We'd do well to . . . perform those few sacred offices for which we've been chosen by God, and forget the rest. Oh, of course, we're entitled to a little harmless relaxation. And, whatever else we do, let's not put ourselves between God and the people—or let them put us between them and Him as too often happens nowadays. . . . Forty years ago, we weren't expected to do so much selling, nagging, and hand-holding" (pp. 142–43).

So, too, the Archbishop of Powers's "Prince of Darkness" further instructs Father Burner in the evils of the overly tolerant, modern Catholic Church when he tells him: "we spend more time listening to the voice of the people than is good for either it or us. We have been too generous with our ears, Father. We have handed over our tongues also. . . . For we square the circle beautifully in almost every country on earth. We bring neither peace nor a sword. The rich give us money. We give them consolation and make of the eye of the needle a gate. Together we try to reduce the Church, the Bride of Christ, to a streetwalker" (pp. 190, 192). The prophets of these Christian works are heroes who have rejected the humanism of the modern age to live solitary lives of simplicity and moral decency.

Walker Percy, then, is at odds, philosophically, with much of the contemporary life reflected so perceptively in his novels. He knows his age well, speaks feelingly in the voice of the modern alienated man, but is not any more "contemporary" in his outlook than either Flannery O'Connor or J. F. Powers. With these two fellow Catholic authors, Percy condemns both present-day American society and a Church he sees as reflecting that society. All three join the Archbishop of "Prince of Darkness" in exposing the progressive, twentieth century Roman Catholic Church as "the Bride of Christ" turned "streetwalker," a Church so worldly that it can be satirized as "Second Only to Standard Oil" in the eighth chapter of *Morte D'Urban*. The prophets of Powers, Percy, and O'Connor become, of necessity, then, martyrs from another time in Church history, disjoined from both contemporary life and modern Christian ecumenicism. "Crazed," sword-bearing, solitary religious fanatics, Lancelot, Father Urban, Tarwater, and Hazel Motes assault the contemporary manners and philosophies of fellow Christians and secularists alike. The sword of "the old Catholic way" they carry is, it seems, for their creators, the only means these Christian heroes have of restoring life to a lost and blinded world.

NOTES

[1]Josephine Hendin, *The World of Flannery O'Connor* (Bloomington, Indiana: Indiana Univ. Press, 1970), pp. 24–25.

[2]Flannery O'Connor, *Wise Blood* in *Three* (New York: Signet, 1960), p. 126. Subsequent references to *Wise Blood* and *The Violent Bear It Away* are to this edition.

[3]J. F. Powers, *Morte D'Urban* (Garden City: Doubleday, 1962), p. 104. Subsequent references are to this edition.

[4]J. F. Powers, "Prince of Darkness" in *Prince of Darkness and Other Stories* (Garden City: Doubleday, 1947), pp. 190–191. Subsequent references are to this edition.

[5]Flannery O'Connor, "Parker's Back," in *Everything That Rises Must Converge* (New York: Signet, 1967), p. 198.

Lancelot and the Medieval Quests
of
Sir Lancelot and Dante

CORINNE DALE

When a self-proclaimed messiah prophesies the destruction of modern corruption and proclaims a new life of pastoral harmony, we are inclined to be skeptical. Our uneasiness increases when he describes his conception of present decadence—"the secret of life is violence and rape, and its gospel is pornography" (*L.*, p. 224)—and when he asserts his intolerant vision of the future—"no Russkies or Chinks" (p. 256). But what if he announces that he himself will forcibly inaugurate the new age? When he backs up his threat with the story of his first messianic act—the murder of his wife, her lover, and two friends—and when he describes himself as the New Adam accompanied by his New Eve—a social worker who, he claims, has been purified by a gang-rape—our suspicions are confirmed: the man belongs in a nuthouse.

A nuthouse, or "Center for Aberrant Behavior," is where *Lancelot* takes place, and the self-proclaimed messiah, this madman and murderer, is the protagonist, Lancelot Andrewes Lamar. Lance has a point: the society he describes is corrupt, deadened by pills and booze and sex. But isn't he himself a symptom rather than a saviour? Lance considers the lax sexual standards of modern times the chief symptom of moral deterioration. The home movies he makes for evidence of his wife's infidelity show his sixteen year old daughter's ménage à trois and his wife's progression from lover to lover. But surely these pornographic films are no better than the commercial movies which Lance despises. Because he reasons that love can be both the greatest evil and the greatest good, he has become obsessed with sexual sin, seeking assurance of good through knowledge of "a purely evil deed,

99

an intolerable deed for which there is no explanation" (p. 52). Failing to find evidence of pure evil, he intends to found a chivalric society in which he himself will determine tolerable and intolerable behavior. Like other of Percy's protagonists, Lance is a seeker, a questing spirit among anaesthetized souls and one who dares to plunge into the "heart of darkness" (p. 216). But Lance's quest is unholy; his method, destructive; and his dream, the raving of a madman.

Still, we cannot simply dismiss Lance as a lunatic. At the end of the novel, having been proclaimed psychiatrically fit and legally innocent, he is released from his cell and intends to set out for Virginia to plot the bloody revolution he foresees. Moreover, he is not alone in his cell: a rather mysterious figure, a priest-physician and childhood friend, visits him there, eliciting the narration which comprises the novel. This visitor, although for the most part silent, endorses Lance's prophecy of a new life in Virginia, but not necessarily the new life which Lance envisions. The visitor also indicates that he has a message—a message which will be uttered, however, only after the novel ends. At the close of the last chapter we finally hear the visitor speak, if only in monosyllabic responses to Lance's questions. Looking Lance full in the face to indicate that he has something of importance to communicate, the visitor replies to Lance's final query, " 'Is there anything you wish to tell me before I leave?' *'Yes'* " (p. 257). And there the novel ends.

This unheard message, anticipated from the beginning, is absolutely crucial to the reader's satisfaction. The ending, moreover, is not so much ambiguous as unfinished; that is, Percy relies on the reader to supply the final message in order to qualify Lance's projection of the future and to resolve the question raised about the nature of love. Can he really expect to establish a dichotomized society in which men will be either gentlemen or thieves and women either ladies or whores? If not, what will his new life be? The reader, placed in the position of the confessor, cannot avoid the nagging conviction that the unheard sentence is accessible, the inevitable response to the confession which we, as listeners, should know. This feeling of near-recognition, fostered by our identification with the silent visitor, is not misleading. Percy does not tantalize us merely for the sake of suspense; the answer is available—is, in fact, contained in the structure of the novel.

It is impossible to ignore the structural parallels of Lance's story to the quest of Malory's Sir Lancelot du Lac. Lance himself acknowledges the similarity, describing his search for sexual sin as his Unholy Grail. He often compares himself to King Arthur's knight, declaring that he was actually named after Sir Lancelot rather than after the Anglican divine, the Andrewes having been tacked on to his name in the attempt to give it Episcopal sanction. And Lance calls his visitor Percival from a childhood nickname. Most significantly, the Grail legend explores the conflict of secular and spiritual love similar to the conflict of sensual and chivalrous love which torments Lance. Lance is sometimes confused about the details of the quest for the Holy Grail: for example, he states that only two knights achieve the Grail, forgetting that Galahad, Sir Lancelot's son, is also successful. Nevertheless, the structural similarities in the two stories are extensive.

Both Lancelots are aristocratic champions of the poor and oppressed, Lance having worked with blacks during the sixties for civil rights. Like Sir Lancelot, Lance initially enjoys an innocent love affair: Sir Lancelot's love for Guinivere in the first part of his story is sanctioned by the courtly love tradition, and Lance remembers his first marriage with Lucy as a time of innocence. Both Lancelots indulge in a later period of sensuality: Sir Lancelot spent two years at Joyous Isle with Elaine, their child, her father, and a troop of maidens and knights: Lance lived at his Louisiana mansion, Belle Isle, with his second wife Margot, their daughter, Margot's father, and the troop of Hollywood people who are making a film there.

Furthermore, the two Lancelots seem to have lapsed into a trance-like state during this period—Lance calls it a "dream state" (p. 57)—in which they half-consciously play the roles offered them by their environments and by their companions, states from which they are suddenly awakened. Lance likens himself to Sir Lancelot at the moment when he comes to himself in the woods after being caught in adultery with the queen. Lance, however, admits that "it's a bad comparison" (p. 64), especially since Lance is the cuckold not the adulterer. In fact, Lance more closely resembles Sir Lancelot at the moment when Percival recognizes him at Joyous Isle, where he has been living in disguise. Subsequently, Percival takes him back to

Camelot where he is inspired by the Grail to renounce his impure life and set out on his quest. Percy's Lance, having discovered his wife's infidelity by chance, is also awakened to a perception of his wasted life at Belle Isle. Lance acknowledges that he has become a mere creature of habit and dissolution, a mediocre and middle class man, and decides to reform, to become an avenging hero. Just as this stage of entranced physical love in Sir Lancelot's life is ended when he begins his quest for the Holy Grail, Lance also begins a new life of renunciation in his quest for the Unholy Grail, sexual sin. At the end of their searches, both experience the blast of an explosion: Sir Lancelot is knocked out for twenty-four hours when he attempts to enter the room in which the Grail is present, and Percy's unholy knight is caught in the explosion which he has set to destroy his mansion and the people in it.

At this point the stories begin to diverge and, in fact, to oppose one another. Lance's quest is, after all, inverted: he is the knight of the Unholy Grail, and he proposes a return to chivalry, the secular life which Sir Lancelot finally rejects. Lance evades the question of an all-encompassing Christian love: "Don't talk to me of love until we shovel out the shit" (p. 179). As Lance's confession has progressed, the priest-physician, like the medieval Percival, has gained religious strength: he dons priest's clothing during the course of the year and near the end of the novel says a prayer for the dead, a service which he has earlier refused. Moreover, Lance calls him Christ and Jesus— epithets which are disguised as expletives but which still carry religious impact. Yet Lance refuses to hear the visitor's spiritual counsel, rejecting a merciful love which could bridge the gap between the imperfect real world and the chivalric life which he envisions. Unlike Sir Lancelot, who is torn between secular and religious love, Lance makes a distinction between two types of human love—sexual and chivalric love. This crucial difference accounts for the inversion at the climax of the two otherwise similar stories. Unlike Sir Lancelot, Lance fails to accomplish his quest. "There is no unholy grail just as there was no Holy Grail" (p. 253), he decides.

In spite of this failure and the numbness which Lance experiences instead of a sense of revelation, he plans to establish a new life based on chivalry in contrast to the religious life embraced by Sir Lancelot.

And his visitor, who intends to take a church in Alabama just as the medieval Percival enters a hermitage outside the city, confirms Lance's projection of a new life in Virginia with Anna, the rape victim. The reader, however, cannot accept Lance's vision of the future without misgivings, not only because he proposes an impossible return to a mythical chivalric age based on the legendary Old South but also because he espouses violence and what is surely a merciless and distorted view of modern life. Declaring that the secret of love is hate, Lance equates human love with rape. Humans exist, he believes, "for one end and one end only: to commit a sexual assault on another human or to submit to such an assault" (p. 222). This conflict between what the novel seems to affirm and the reader's humanistic values is disconcerting. But here lies the importance of the unheard sentence—the visitor's message. Lance's revelation, unlike that of Sir Lancelot, is yet to come.

The nature of this revelation is suggested by another structural parallel, invoked by Percy in the following inscription which prefaces the novel:

> He sank so low that all means
>   for his salvation were gone,
>   except showing him the lost people.
> For this I visited the region of the dead. . . .

This passage from the *Purgatorio* suggests a parallel to the quest of Dante, another great medieval seeker also concerned with the relationship of secular and spiritual love (cf. the discussion in Coles, *Walker Percy*). Dante's first pure love ended abruptly with the death of Beatrice just as Lucy's early death terminated the pure love stage of Lance's life. Later Dante apparently also indulged in a hedonistic life, since the heavenly Beatrice chides him for forsaking his pure morality to plunge into wickedness after her death. Just as Lance has found himself " 'in the dark' " (p. 5), Dante at the opening of *The Divine Comedy* suddenly finds himself in the midst of a dark wood. Lance's visitor, a friend from the past, resembles Dante's guide, the ghost of Virgil: he appears from the cemetery on All Soul's Day and is several times likened to a ghost, and he finally breaks a long silence to guide Lance through the realms of the dead—his past—and to accompany him through Purgatory—his year in the mental hospital.

As the inscription explains, Dante is shown the damned souls in order to prepare him for the revelation which follows. Percy makes it clear that Lance, too, needs a guide, someone to focus his attention on the past. Lance protests that the past is not meaningful and that he cannot remember it, but clearly he cannot fully comprehend the visitor's message until he has thoroughly examined the motives and emotions which accompanied his crime. Several times during the course of the narrative, the visitor starts to speak but hesitates and instead redirects Lance's attention to this crucial point in his past. And in spite of his protests, Lance himself knows that something went wrong with his life and that the past holds a clue.

In the memories of his past, Lance finds his own carnal hell on earth, and Lance's hell bears a striking resemblance to Dante's second circle, which Lance refers to as "a rather pleasant anteroom to hell" (p. 17). It is here, incidentally, that Dante meets Paolo and Francesca, the lovers who were inspired to commit sexual sin by reading of Lancelot's and Guinivere's first kiss. In Dante's second circle, carnal lovers are driven about incessantly in total darkness by fierce winds. The events which Lance recalls take place in a similar environment. The moviemakers at Belle Isle have simulated a hurricane as background for the x-rated film they are making, a film which features a sexual saviour who transforms all evil to erotic good. This simulated hurricane is soon overwhelmed by hurricane Marie, whom the revellers greet with an orgy of sex and drugs. Moreover, the videotapes commissioned by Lance in order to view the sexual antics of his wife are distorted so that "The figures seemed to be blown in an electronic wind" (p. 185). The Belle Isle of Lance's memories is indeed a carnal hell.

To discover the clue in the past, Lance must review not only the events of the past but also his own emotions. The visitor again and again speaks of love, asking Lance if he loved Margot and finally if he can ever love anyone. (We infer these questions from Lance's responses, since the visitor remains silent until near the end.) Tormented by Margot's infidelity, by the fact that she has physically loved another man, Lance parries the question, refusing to call sexual passion love. But at the same time, he describes his joy with Margot in such loving detail that there is little doubt. Dichotomizing love into chivalrous and sensual love, he declares that in the future men "will know which women are to be fucked and which to be honored and one will know who to fuck and who to honor" (p. 179). But Margot's dying words indicate the error of this severe judgment: "With you I had to be either—or—but never a—uh—woman" (p. 245).

By reviewing the past with the priest as his guide, Lance has come to recognize that his quest has failed: instead of experiencing a sense of absolute sin at the end of his quest, he has discovered only numbness. As the novel closes, he is still in his purgatorial cell. He complains of being cold, unable to feel emotion, and he continues to describe things with a cold logic which belies emotional involvement. But there are suggestions of the change to come.

The inscription chosen by Percy locates Lance at the end of his purgatory, recalling the moment when Virgil surrenders Dante to the guidance of Beatrice. As Beatrice looks Dante directly in the eyes for the first time, her brilliant gaze reveals to him the light of heaven. In *Lancelot* it is the visitor who looks straight at Lance before revealing the truth to him, and this visitor has been called Lance's Beatrice. The visitor admits, however, that his message is not important since what he has to say will happen anyway. In *The Divine Comedy*, too, the Church fails as a guide to spiritual fulfillment; it is human love which proves regenerative to Dante, and it is human love which must transform Lance. The priest-visitor will soon be replaced as a guide by Anna, the rape victim, who is repeatedly compared to Lucy, Lance's first love. This "Lucy of the new world" (p. 86) is almost a reincarnation of his first wife so that Lance rediscovers his first innocent love just as Dante finds Beatrice once more. And like Beatrice, Anna can show Lance what the priest can only verbalize.

When Lance invites Anna to join him she refuses to commit herself because he cannot say that he loves her, and later she angrily denies that the secret of life is "the ignominious joy of rape and being raped" (p. 252). She inserts a welcome note of sanity when she rejects his notion that her ordeal has either violated or purged her inner self. In spite of these rejections, however, Anna, according to the visitor, will accompany Lance to Virginia. Clearly, her presence will modify Lance's plan for a chivalric society in which sensual love will be divorced from "pure" love. Anna, like Margot before her, denies this scheme of absolutes. In spite of her rape, she refuses to consider sex a force of evil. Like Beatrice, she can reveal to Lance what the priest could not: the transforming power of human love.

By suspending Lance between the moments of revelation of the two great medieval seekers, Percy provides the key to the unheard message at the end of *Lancelot*. Lance recalls Sir Lancelot at the end of the *Sangreal* just as he suggests Dante at the end of the *Purgatorio*. But Lance's search for the Unholy Grail is not rewarded; the revelation is pending. Like Dante at the moment indicated by the inscription, Lance is on the brink of a discovery. The movie made at Belle Isle foretells this revelation. Although it focuses rather crudely on the sexual aspect of human love, it shows "that the girl with her own gift for tenderness and caring converts a moment of violence into a moment of love. . . . The girl guides him toward life through the erotic. She is his Beatrice" (p. 114).

Lancelot:
Sign for the Times

JEROME C. CHRISTENSEN

"... peculiar times require peculiar quests."

Walker Percy's *Lancelot*, a very peculiar book, engages the critic, challenges his stance, in the way few contemporary American novels any longer care to do. *Lancelot* is the monologue—now obstreperous, now canny, now frightening, now pathetic—of a madman, the tale of a brutal negative quest, brutally told. Mad Lancelot surely is, but mad in a fashion that blunts the critic's diagnostic instrument and subverts his presumption of sane and sanitary distance, for the symmetry between the narrator's violently obsessive quest for meaning through his telling and the critic's zealous and equally over-determined pursuit of meaning in the tale is inescapable and disturbing. Is it not mad to monograph on a madman's monologue? That question identifies the predicament that is *Lancelot*—a predicament especially pointed for criticism but implicated in any authentic reading of the novel. *Lancelot* is a novel about a character in a predicament; ultimately that character is I—reader and writer.

Most Americans are well acquainted with the disadvantages of madness: the delicate wariness that settles in on the faces of relatives and friends; the irksome difficulty in keeping the golf card straight; a certain moroseness that taints one's enjoyment of even the most tasteful serials on PBS; a persistent itch beyond the power of Downy Fabric Softener to allay. But if we are almost tediously familiar with the disadvantages of madness, perhaps we are insufficiently aware of its advantages. Chief among them is the possibility *of* a vantage, a point of view. It may be a slight vantage, as narrow as the view from the window of a madhouse; but, as Lancelot Andrewes Lamar, madman,

107

attests to his silent interlocuter, "the narrower the view, the more you can see" (p. 3). What Lancelot sees out the window of his New Orleans madhouse is "a patch of sky, a corner of Lafayette Cemetery, a slice of levee, and a short stretch of Annunciation Street" (pp. 3–4), and, he tells us, part of a sign. It reads:

Free &
Ma
B

For the madman the fragment lures speculation. Lancelot freely conjectures what the whole sign might say: "Free & Easy Mac's Bowling? Free & Accepted Masons' Bar?" (p. 4). He expects to learn the answer when, after finally proving his sanity, he leaves his confinement. And maybe he will, though the novel ends in the delay of that departure and that discovery. I won't ever know what the complete sign says, unless I should be very lucky and on a future trip to New Orleans find such a sign on such a street. What a bonus for sanity that would be! The narrow view of the novel divulges only a partial sign, however, and, in doing so, simultaneously poses and answers the riddle, when is a sign not merely a sign? The answer: when it is a message, when it addresses me in my predicament, even if its only address is "you are in a predicament"—when, that is, I am forced to make use of it because I have nothing else (see *MB*, pp. 119–49). In my predicament as reader of this book, provided with only a narrow view between its red walls, the insignificant breaks upon me with the force of a message, even if that message conveys only the urgency of my questions: *Free* and what? What does *Ma* have to do with it? *B*? What? How? This must be madness.

Free &

Freedom, as Lancelot's favorite song says, is just another word for nothing left to lose. Lancelot's madness began with the sudden awareness of that freedom in the shocking recognition of nothing. From his vantage in the madhouse Lancelot tells his story, the tale of a Louisiana lawyer in his forties, squire of the family mansion of Belle Isle, a former happy hedonist whose pleasures have lost their savour. Lancelot's second wife, Margot, has made a rapid transit from *nouveau riche* to *nouveau* antiquarian; she begins by restoring Belle Isle to its antebellum splendor, tries to restore her husband to a likeness of Jefferson Davis, and turns, finally, to the project of restoring herself to a factitious glamour by becoming a motion picture actress. As if by the logic of that restoration Lancelot has been eased out of the revived grandeur of his ancestral home into the pigeonnier out back, where he roosts, a lone pigeon, while a flock of Hollywood moviemakers on location nest in the manse. Always a creature of habits, Lancelot has by now been reduced to just three: drinking, reading Raymond Chandler, and, preeminently, monitoring the news. Every pleasantly pickled hour he listens to the reports on the radio, and every evening his last, ritualistic act is to cast a blood-dimmed eye on the television's spectral summary of the day's events: no-news from everywhere. He does not realize his compulsiveness or his discontent until, one afternoon, he suddenly *does* receive news, from a wholly unexpected source, in a form not immediately explicable but immediately meaningful. The message: nothing. Or, to be more precise: oh, cipher, zero. Looking up from a Chandler novel, Lancelot glances at a release form for his daughter's summer camp and notices that her blood type is listed as I-0. That 0, the place-saver in the decimal system, when placed behind the one and the hyphen, simultaneously indicates his daughter's blood-type and displaces Lancelot with his IV-AB from her blood-line, involving the giddy inference that he has been replaced in his wife's bed. Lancelot retrospectively compares the effect of this discovery to the insistent and catastrophic chain of inferences that follow upon an astronomer's observation of the dislodgment of a single point of light in a galaxy trillions of miles away: "The astronomer sees a dot in the wrong place, makes a calculation, and infers the indisputable: comet on collision course, tidal waves, oceans rising, forests ablaze. The cuckold sees a single letter of the alphabet in the wrong place. From such insignificant evidence he can infer with at least as much certitude as the astronomer an equally incommensurate scene: his wife's thighs spread, a cry, not recognizably hers, escaping her lips. The equivalent of the end of the world following upon the out-of-place dot is her ecstasy inferred from the O" (pp. 20–21).

A violent logic, which will, for Lancelot, justify violence. Violent, but if mad, it is the madness of our own Judaeo-Christian culture, which becomes intelligible only in the plausibility of the end of the world and in the possibility of moral and spiritual equivalents to the eschaton. And, given the end of the world, a certain violent logic does enforce itself: because the eschaton will be a unique and totalizing event, it must be incommensurate with anything else, context or cause. For both astronomer and cuckold to follow the chain of inferences that unveils the end of the world requires a transcendental leap from the general to the unique, from evidence to experience, from mild interest to fierce passion. It follows that the truest moral equivalent to the eschaton emerges where incommensurability is both most familiar and least intelligible, in the sexual climax, which, as Lancelot argues, belongs to none of our conventional categories and which is, properly speaking, *unspeakable*. The incommensurability of the sexual orgasm, which in its *ek stasis* takes one out of one's place, opens to an absolute beyond the phenomenal—an absolute, Lancelot insists, either infinitely good or infinitely evil. The only anchor available to stabilize this indeterminate moment is fidelity; fidelity between the partners to this grave ecstasy is the life preserving fiction of a benign commensurability. For Lancelot to suddenly infer the entirely separate ecstasy of his wife from the out-of-place, unfaithful *O* is to cut away that stabilizing anchor and to chart will he nill he a course to the end of the line: to sheer negativity, absolute evil. Such is the logic of eschatology, wherein the world is ultimately consumed not because of a stray comet but because of its own incommensurate, fatal significance.

Suddenly, giddily free, with nothing left to lose, Lancelot seems to come to himself, feels capable of action for the first time in many years. The inference of absolute evil does have, like madness, its compensations: it makes knights out of broken down old boozers, and it imparts a kind of heady joy in the heart of despair—what Lancelot calls a "secret sweetness at the core of dread" (p. 41). Lancelot describes that peculiar emotion by comparing the discovery of his wife's infidelity to the time when, as a child, he accidentally came upon a cache of 10,000 embezzled dollars buried beneath the argyle socks in his father's bureau—evidence of an unsuspected corruption that knocked the son's world to pieces. He recalls the hunger of his eyes for the sight of that dirty money, how they shifted to and fro ever so slightly, scanning, gluttonously trying to take it all in. Lancelot feels the same sweet dread in the evidence of his wife's ecstasy. Opening to his eye, the O provokes what Lancelot calls the "worm of interest" (p. 21), which, once stimulated, will wriggle into an emptiness at one and the same time repellent and inviting. For the worm, inference is but appetizer. Though vengeance be Lancelot's goal, he must satisfy the interested eye by feasting on the act itself in the absolute knowledge of whether all is good or evil, niceness or buggery.

In his pursuit of this awful knowledge Lancelot eccentrically emulates the method of Philip Marlowe, tarnished knight in the city of fallen angels. The man becomes the private I; private eye turns peeper. He first enlists the services of his black factotum Elgin (the name of a watch) to observe and chart the comings and goings of the film crew at the local Holiday Inn. When the evidence of bedhopping proves inconclusive, Lancelot, with the help of Elgin's MIT-trained expertise, sophisticates his methods, substituting for his servant's eyes the objective probing lens of the camera. After insuring that the film company will have to spend their last two nights at Belle Isle, he converts the house into a weird television studio, each bedroom equipped with its own prosthetic eyeball. But the more sophisticated the equipment, the more bizarre the results. This technique of bringing the sinners into focus with movement-activated cameras and infrared lenses does show them compromised but in a compromise of the viewing instrument itself, which records them strangely distorted—a so-called negative effect that aptly comments on Lancelot's negative quest.

Furious to eliminate the indeterminacy that haunts him, Lancelot decides to feast his eyes directly on the truth. He prepares for a vengeance that will be identical with knowledge, where the hidden evil will be raped by a sovereign knower. The next evening he diverts gas from a partially capped well into the ventilation system of the sealed house and then balefully enters its poisonous darkness. The cold eye of the hurricane that rages without, Lancelot pierces ever deeper into the bedrooms of those who sport in adultery and perversions, until, at the center, he ruthlessly lances the infections with penis and knife in a violent knowledge that discloses the secret of life and affirms the justice of his quest even as the apocalyptic explosion of the gas-filled house affirms the intelligibility of history itself.

Apocalypse may have come, but Lancelot, survivor, is no less haunted. By recounting his terrible story to a priest/physician and former friend he seeks to regain a lost focus and assurance, to rediscover a truth he is sure he knows. In this narrative quest the mind wends its way through a lurid landscape oppressively charged with significance. The madman's compact with lover and poet is to compare great things with small. And as Lancelot has inferred absolute evil from the evidence of his wife's infidelity, so does he find in his predicament the type of an evil that has correspondences everywhere. Whether or not the world has actually ended or will end, the need for an end and for a new beginning is starkly legible in the signs of the times. The madman's litany of those signs builds to a wholesale denunciation of the homogenized hell of contemporary America: "Washington, the country, is down the drain. Everyone knows it. The people have lost it to the politicians, bureaucrats, drunk Congressmen, lying Presidents, White House preachers, C.I.A., F.B.I., Mafia, Pentagon, pornographers, muggers, buggers, bribers, bribe takers, rich crooked cowboys, sclerotic Southerners, rich crooked Yankees, dirty books, dirty movies, dirty plays, dirty talk shows, dirty soap operas, fags, lesbians, abortionists, Jesus shouters, anti-Jesus shouters, dying cities, dying schools, courses in how to fuck for schoolchildren" (p. 220).

The loss of the country is the surrender to spectacle; the task of living has become a business of show. And show business— Hollywood movies and moviemakers—becomes for Lancelot the epitome of a pervasive, disgusting infidelity of appearance to reality. A century ago Walt Whitman stood on California's shores and saw the great westering circle almost circled. Just twenty years ago Alan Ginsberg wandered through a supermarket in California and found *both* peaches *and* penumbras. Today, Lancelot envisions a California where a movie theater playing *Deep Throat* snuggles knowingly up to the gates of San Clemente—the Hollywood version of Paradise, where the hypocrite will lie down with the pornographer. Worse, in the inevitable reflex of sin, Hollywood, with its hurricane machines and freeze-dried divinities, has spread east, where actors and actresses, producers and directors mindlessly spout the ideology of a joyful, life-enhancing sexuality while they secretly practice fornication and buggery in lewd daisy chains that are the perversion of nature. As it must, the diseased part infects the whole: Lamia—fantastic, alluring—first poisons the bed and then one's hold on reality itself: "The world had gone crazy, said the crazy man in his cell. What was nutty was that the movie folk were trafficking in illusions in a real world but the real world thought that its reality could only be found in the illusions" (p. 152). The proper equivalent of this nutty indeterminacy is not the liberal's daydream of a pluralist society fondly tolerant of all distinctions, but Pandaemonium, Mammon's mimic kingdom—a hellish nightmare which threatens to make all distinctions impossible. One choice alone remains: to settle into that ultimate form of alienation that Blake called the limit of opacity or to elect a Luciferian indignation which in acknowledging a fallen estate insists nonetheless on the prerogatives of a proud sovereignty.

As his indignant answer to this intolerable age of Sodom Lancelot envisions a new order of things where sovereignty is possible, a place and time of capable action. He prophesies a revolution. "You have your Sacred Heart," he tells the priest. "We have Lee. We are the Third Revolution. The First Revolution in 1776 against the stupid British succeeded. The Second Revolution in 1861 against the money-grubbing North failed—as it should have because we got stuck with the Negro thing and it was our fault. The Third Revolution will succeed" (p. 157). Lancelot's prophecy corrects the American myth of the ever new frontier by identifying it as the mere rotation of keenly felt, constrictive limits with the comforting illusion of the limitless. (On rotation and reversal, see *MB*, pp. 83–100.) In its stead he projects a myth of return, to Virginia, beautiful island between North and South, where America began, where will congregate a band of gentlemen, militant in their assured virtue, disciplined by the knightly values of "tight-lipped courtesy between men. And chivalry toward women," whom the men will save "from the whoredom they've chosen" (p. 158). The stern Virginian will fashion from *Free & O* (open, type 0, type and archetype, aught and naught) the noble prospect for a sanely limited community. Lancelot quotes inspiringly from the traditional song:

Oh, Columbia, our blessed mother
You know we wait until you guide us.
Give us a sign and march beside us. (p. 221)

The curve of Lancelot's madness is the impassioned trajectory from the misplaced *0* tickling his worm of interest to this vision of Columbia chastely offering a transparent sign of noble purpose to her marching sons.

And what of Columbia's daughters? What will their freedom be? Lancelot is explicit: "They will have the freedom to be a Lady or a Whore"—a single, determinate choice, on which the whole vision rests, for that determinacy is anchored in the great secret of life which was the unholy prize of Lancelot's quest. "The great secret of the ages," he reveals, "is that man has evolved, is born, lives, and dies for one end and one end only: to commit a sexual assault on another human or to submit to such an assault" (p. 222). He goes on later: "God's secret design for man is that man's happiness lies for men in men practicing violence upon women and that woman's happiness lies in submitting to it" (p. 224). Given that brutal design, the distinction between lady and whore is simply a reflection of the determinate difference between fidelity and betrayal. The news that in this fallen world such a distinction can and must be made is the grail that Lancelot has brought back from the end of the world. As an answer to the priest's pious objection that we have been redeemed, Lancelot disdainfully gestures to his narrow view and says, "Look out there. Does it look like we are redeemed?" (p. 224).

Can this view be controverted? Try. It's like arguing with a madman. A madman with a sword. Would it do any good to suggest that this vision of a reactionary revolution is actually a repetition, to point out that Southern men have already banded together as a clan of knights sworn to chivalric protection of the pure Southern Lady? Almost certainly not, for in his madness Lancelot knows what we Sodomites do not guess, that in the hazards of true repetition lies the only possibility of raising alienated consciousness to the second power, a secondary reflection which in its difference identifies the mind's potential sovereignty and freedom (see *MB*, p. 96). This power of repetition is attested to by the major repetitions in the book: the repetition of the quest of the original Lancelot by his namesake; the repetition of the quest of the latter-day knight in his monologue. One must return in order to begin. In repetition is the possibility of action and knowledge.

But repetition is also the limit of action and knowledge. One can plan a Virginian garden of Adamic freedom; but, as we know, the limit of Adam is Eve. Lancelot chooses as his Eve, Anna, the woman in the next cell, who has been reduced by gang rape to near catatonia and whom he involves in various fantasies of communication and conjugation. When recovered, however, she shatters those fantasies in her climactic rejection of his vision of Gentleman Adam and Lady Eve, sovereign raper and submissive rapee. "Are you suggesting," she cries, "that I, myself, me, my person, can be violated by a *man*? You goddamn men. Don't you know that there are more important things in this world? Next you'll be telling me that despite myself I liked it" (p. 251). Her angry response, proclaiming an absolute resistance to violation by a self open to more important things, disrupts the delicate focus of Lancelot's monologue and repeats a disturbance that, he realizes, occurred earlier—on the night of his vengeance and in the heart of his triumph. There, at the end of the line, his unfaithful wife Margot, the ark of covenant that bears his unholy grail, speaks to him in a poignant, etherized dismay about the losses of their lives. Just before the final conflagration she asks, "What's the matter with me?" "What?" he responds. "That's what you never knew," she says. "With you I had to be either—or—but never a—uh—woman. It was good for a while" (p. 245). Her last words are less important than her last silences. The rapee turns on the raper in the moment of his knowledge with a gentle accusation that is the dying echo of a lost possibility: you never knew; I had to be either—or—but never a—uh—woman. The pauses mark the limits of Lancelot's knowledge: either a lady or a whore but never a woman. And what he hears, he sees. In the flaring of the last match Lancelot can see his wife in the corner "lying on her side," as he tells it, "like Anna, knees drawn up, cheek against her hands pressed palms together, dark eyes gazing at me" (pp. 245–46). At the end of the line the knower looks into the sweet secret of dread and sees that secret looking back at him.

The limit of Adam may be Eve, but what does

Ma

have to do with it? The limit of Lancelot, as we know from Malory, is Lancelot, who is both his virtue *and* his taint. The unexpected memory of Margot and the rejection by Anna rupture Lancelot's narrative like the return of the repressed, releasing the confession that his quest had failed after all, that he never found the secret knowledge he has professed. Instead of whore or rapee he has come upon a woman staring at him in sympathy or shouting at him in rage—each encounter marking the beam in his own hungry eye. This failure and its consequent repression occur because this hero is not only Lancelot but Lancelot Andrewes Lamar, son of a dreamy, impotent country squire, who just happens to be a crook, and of Lily of Belle Isle, frail and pretty, who just happens, it seems (the evidence is inferential), to be an adultress with jovial Uncle Harry. As Lancelot repeatedly recalls, the primal scene of infidelity lay in his childhood discovery of the dirty money hidden in the cavity of his father's sock drawer, the moment when he first experienced the wild surmise that would later prompt him to his unholy quest. But what of Ma? As it was his mother who sent him (wittingly or unwittingly?) on that first unknowing journey to the uncanny secret—sign of dishonor and impotence—in his father's drawer, so it is his mother who appears in a vision as Joan of Arc to offer him the sword, or at least the Bowie knife, of vengeance at the fatal hour. But if it is his mother as Lady whom Lancelot is avenging, it is also his mother as Whore on whom he is taking vengeance. For it is his mother's uncertain fidelity which is the type of that indeterminacy between Lady and Whore that Lancelot aims to extirpate. He rouses himself from a stupor like his father's and attempts to save himself from the emasculation involved in his father's substitution of the bundle of bright, green money for the fact of a female sexuality too darkly, sweetly dreadful to confront. In attempting to free himself from his father's impotent trance, however, Lancelot obsessively repeats his father's self-destructive evasions. Fantasizing his mother as Joan of Arc, militant virgin, and accepting from her hands the prosthetic penis of the Bowie knife is an arming every bit as unmanning as his father's disarming retreat into genteel avarice. If his father dishonored himself by substituting the corrupt image of money for the uncanniness of his wife's cunt, then Lancelot repeats that error in his substitution of the fascinating uncanniness of the cunt for the vital indeterminacy of the woman. The measure of Lancelot's ambivalence is the impossibility of a man ever knowing absolutely whether his mother is a lady or a whore. The motive of his action is the incapacity of *this* man ever to accept her as a woman. By finding and sacrificing the actual whore, be it Margot or Hollywood, he hopes to save the memory of his mother—Joan of Arc, Columbia, America herself—as Lady. It never works.

Now I *am* in a predicament. I can, if I choose, yield to the momentum of my argument and reasonably explain away Lancelot's rant by psychoanalyzing him, reducing his unsettling vision of America, of man and woman, to the wholly understandable consequence of childhood trauma. From that perspective all that stuff about the end of the world is merely more of the same. Repetition is the limit of action and knowledge. But the monstrous excellence of this book is that though Percy generously supplies the material and tools for such a reduction, he cannily prohibits any comfort in its execution. If I, rationalist, substitute a bright, tidy psychoanalytic explanation for Lancelot's eccentric narrative, I merely repeat his obsessive quest for the determinate and thereby commit myself to a monologue mad like his but chilling and sterile. Every man has a Ma, but only Lancelot tells this disturbing story.

Repetition is the possibility of action and knowledge. That possibility is realized in the book through the development of the figure who listens to Lancelot's story. A priest/physician, what Lancelot calls either "screwed-up priest or half-assed physician" (p. 10), he is a childhood friend of Lancelot's, who has been known by many names. Called Percival, for the knight "who found the Grail and brought life to a dead land," he visits the tomb of Lancelot where he must both discover and exercise his powers of rejuvenation. Called Pussy, he represents the hard chance that man may come to terms not only with woman but also with the femininity that is part of his own make-up. Called John, he must identify himself as either "John the Evangelist who loved so much or John the Baptist, a loner out in the wilderness" (p. 10). While listening to Lancelot this man, "neither fish nor fowl" (p. 5) when the monologue begins, passes from a state of abstraction to an exploratory interest, and finally to a difficult commitment both to

Lancelot and to a renewed religious faith—a commitment quietly
signaled by the priest's hesitation in the cemetery outside Lancelot's
narrow window as he stops, stoops, to pray for the dead: for Lancelot,
for himself, for me. Percival does not bring his grail to a dead land; he
finds his grail in the broken quest and the tormented narrative of
Lancelot. The priest/physician who aimed to give therapy receives
instead news of, in, and for his predicament. And what he receives he
charitably returns. When Lancelot, in the madness of his lucidity, light
without warmth, exclaims that he is cold (p. 253), it is John the
Evangelist who responds, not simply to comfort Lancelot in his chill,
but to rescue him from what the poet of *Paradise Lost* called "the
bitter change/Of fierce extremes, extremes by change more fierce,/
From Beds of raging Fire, to starve in Ice/[His] soft Ethereal warmth."
The priest responds to Lancelot's implied question,

B

be what? how?, with the promise of a message, of good news.

That news is never spoken. But the signs of the text, however
partial, support, even demand a conjecture. The news must be the
hardly possible alternative to both the intolerable Sodom of contemporary America and the mad, murderous rage of Lancelot. It is the
alternative that the priest has been advancing all along: first auto-
matically, then guiltily, then cautiously, and, finally, with an authority
that leaves Lancelot and the reader hanging on his words: love. Love
earned by ordeal, offered in risk, justified by a mortal need. Not *just*
love, but *Christian* love. Lancelot had justified his quest for sure
knowledge of pure sin as a negative proof of God. "If," he had said,
"there is such a thing as sin, *evil*, a living malignant force, there *must*
be a God" (italics added, p. 52). The new sovereignty of man that
Lancelot had envisioned would have been the earthly analogue of the
stern dominion of a divine father. Absolute knowledge forestalled, so
is the sovereignty of God and the certainty of his potent justice. But
the indeterminacy that remains, clarified by trial and refined by need
represents the existential possibility of Christ and his redemptive
love: a love whose incarnation is the revived fraternal affection of
Percival for Lancelot, and whose prospective images are the charity of

a priest in Alabama and the family of man, woman, and daughter in the mountains of Virginia.

That message of love is, as I've said, not spoken in this text. Indeed Lancelot has contemptuously commanded his Percival, "Don't speak to me of Christian love" (p. 158). The priest obeys; he speaks only a series of reassuring "yeses" at the close, affirmations that are not statements but *acts* of love. Perhaps the message of love cannot be spoken without being rendered as utterly banal. And though it is part of the critic's job to make banal utterances, I do apologize for mine. We can't be too certain, or perhaps I should say certain enough, about this book. Like Lancelot, who does not find the consubstantial sign of evil, who can no longer expect the transparent sign that Columbia has promised her sons, and who never even acts on his determination to leave his cell to finally learn the complete version of

Free &
Ma
B

we must take our messages from broken signs, which may madden us or make us lovers—perhaps madden us *then* make us lovers—in a world which, read rightly, is always balancing precariously between a catastrophic end and a tentative beginning.

I have referred to the monstrous excellence of this book, hardly a novel. The text does open like a novel, pricking the reader's worm of interest and inviting him to penetrate the core, to repeat Lancelot's quest for a final knowledge: reader as raper, book as rapee. But the blandishments of structure and motif betray such a reader; what he finally glimpses is something quite different from the feast he had anticipated. Shockingly intolerant of the conventional enticements, radically skeptical of the sources of its own power, this book rebukes the reader's easy interest and shatters his pretense of detachment by involving him in a repetition of Lancelot's catastrophe, a repetition that is the limit and the possibility of readerly action and knowledge. Fiction and tract, narrative and harangue, *Lancelot* is a book that collapses under the pressure of its message. In its collapse *is* its message. Like the priest who learns a saving love from the disjointed monologue of a madman, I, reader and writer, chastened in my pride, subdued by the "end of the novel," can perhaps hear in the silence of the text an urgent note of distress. This note is not the call of madman or prophet but the plaintive, warning song of a canary (*MB*, p. 101).

Walker Percy:
Eschatology and the Politics of Grace

CECIL L. EUBANKS

Eschatological musings are often characteristic of a disintegrating social order; and the frequency of such observations in the twentieth century has led many to conclude with (among others) Hermann Hesse's Steppenwolf that we are caught "between two ages, two modes of life" with the consequence that we have lost "all power to understand" and have "no standard, no security, no simple acquiescence."[1] A more authoritative statement that the basic nomos of western civilization, the Christian-Platonic conception of the world, is losing its hold upon us is the passionate utterance of Friedrich Nietzsche's madman who carries a lantern through the marketplace in the "bright morning hours" and cries "God is dead, God remains dead, And we have killed him." He enters the churches to sing the *requiem aeternam deo* and when forced to account for such absurdity replies, "What are these churches now if they are not the tombs and sepulchers of God." Alas, the news comes too early; and the madman's astonished listeners stare at him in disbelief. Casting his lantern to the ground he agrees that "deeds require time even after they are done before they can be seen and heard."[2]

It took the Verdun and the Hiroshima of the twentieth century to awaken an increasing chorus of believers in Nietzsche's dictum, among them a number of political and social philosophers who see in "modernity" ample evidence to support the madman's claim. This renaissance of political philosophy in the middle of the twentieth century is not an unexpected phenomenon. If we are in a transitional time, anxiety over the state of our being is likely to be high; and—as in past periods of crisis, of disintegration and change—the scope and depth of philosophical inquiry will increase. Nor is it surprising to find that such a renaissance is accompanied by the voice of the poet (novelist). To the nineteenth century analyses of Nietzsche and Kierkegaard (both of whom were poets), we must add the contemporary pronouncements of Sartre, Camus, Kafka, Marcel and the subject of this essay, Walker Percy.

Walker Percy's art and philosophy begin with and are integrally related to the notion of our being in a transitional age. "The modern age," Percy writes, "began to come to an end when men discovered that they could no longer understand themselves by the theory professed by the age" (*MB*, p. 25). He maintains, in other words, that the age has no "theory of man as man." Percy recognizes, as do many existential phenomenologists, that the behavioral social sciences are lacking in one important respect, namely recognition that "there is a meta-scientific, metacultural reality, an order of being apart from the scientific and cultural symbols with which it is grasped and expressed" (*MB*, p. 242). What is needed is a radically new anthropology informed by both the classificatory and the functional sciences and a "normative science" as well. It is noteworthy that Percy is unwilling to allow the word *science* to name the domain of the positivist empiricists alone. Phenomenology is vigorously empirical also, but in a decidedly subjective fashion. In his essay, "The Symbolic Structure of Interpersonal Process," he insists that what needs to be emphasized in any authentic theory of man is "the intimate relationship between the phenomenological structure of intersubjectivity," of community, and the "empirical event of symbolic behavior." Existential experiences do not occur in a vacuum or in the nether world of black magic. "Rather do they follow upon and, in fact, can be derived only from this very intercourse: one man encountering another man, speaking a word, and through it and between them discovering the world and himself" (*MB*, p. 214). Human beings asserting themselves through the language, through symbols, emerge into the daylight of "consciousness and knowing, of happiness and sadness, of being with and being alone, of being right and being wrong, of being [themselves] and being not [themselves], and of being at home and being a stranger" (*MB*, p. 3).

Like so many existentialists Percy attempts in his theory of language, as well as his novels, to recover the human being from the

Cartesian split of mind and body which dominates much of twentieth century thinking. Percy is, of course, influenced greatly by Kierkegaard in these matters; and his radical anthropology has its base in the Kierkegaardian insistence on individual sovereignty and choice as well as in the Judeo-Christian view of man as the fallen seeker.

As Percy has often said, he writes in "the Christian context," and his theory of man is also modeled after the Judeo-Christian anthropology. He believes that this theory is flexible enough to be adapted to the twentieth century, provided that those who adopt it confront the notion of the Fall. The Christian is always faced with the problem of an estrangement which goes beyond the estrangement attributable to technology, to capitalist competition, and failure to adapt to certain social structures. The "normal," common fate of human beings in the Judeo-Christian tradition is alienation. The human being is a seeker, *homo viator*, exploring its alienation from self, others and God.

With these tools, his "notions" of the unique fallen pilgrim and the skills of the poet, Percy explores modern consciousness and subjects it to the inevitable judgment of the philosopher. Despite the disavowals, he points the way to salvation. Like Nietzsche's madman, he enters and cries, "I seek God! I seek God!" and utters his pronouncements.

"Everydayness is the enemy. No search is possible" (*M*, p. 145). With this lament Binx Bolling names his own existence and that of thousands of others who identify with his estranged condition. As Martin Luschei indicates in his fine book on Percy, the estrangement can be depicted as *inauthenticity, abstraction* and *alltäglichkeit* or *everydayness*,[3] all terms taken from the writings of existentialists like Jean-Paul Sartre, Gabriel Marcel and Kierkegaard. But in framing the contours of a boring, conformist, self-objectified existence, Percy coins his own phrases for that general feeling of disquietude that accompanies modern existence. In *Love in the Ruins* and *The Last Gentleman* there are the noxious particles that "inflame and worsen the secret ills of the spirit and rive the very self from itself" (*LR*, p. 5). And in *Love in the Ruins*, there are the vines, possum grape, scuppernong and poison ivy that are "sprouting in earnest" all over the planet, as well as Dr. More's "attacks of elation and depression," and "occasional seizures of morning terror" (*LR*, p. 11). In "Notes for a Novel

About the End of the World" the matter is put quite simply by the "refugee novelist": "*Something is wrong here; I don't feel good*" (*MB*, p. 106). Ultimately Percy draws from his medical background to give what is the definitive naming. It is, of course, *malaise*, describing both the often indefinable sensation of discomfort (except this time it is spiritual) and giving the implicit warning that such a feeling is frequently the signal for the onset of disease.

Percy's diagnosis of the malaise of modern American society begins in the troubled reflections of Binx, the moviegoer, who sees a thin fog of it descending upon his world, and extends into Will Barrett's turgid confrontation with non-being in *The Last Gentleman*; until by the time of *Love in the Ruins* and *Lancelot* his concern has reached apocalyptic proportions befitting his view that this is indeed the end of the modern era. He announces his fears, like an Old Testament prophet, at the beginning of *Love in the Ruins*, ostensibly the last work in the trilogy on alienation:

> These are bad times.
> Principalities and powers are everywhere victorious. Wickedness flourishes in high places. (*LR*, p. 5)

The malaise, as the prophecy implies, is neither a psychological condition alone nor solely spiritual. Its manifestations and causes are due in part to a social and political pathology. *Percy's diagnosis of alienation is a political diagnosis as well.* The numbing quality of everydayness described in *The Moviegoer* and the "crowd culture" mentality that it depicts are the result of a surrender of autonomy to any form of abstraction, be it impersonation of others, the consumption of goods, ideological thinking or bureaucratic indifference. *Percy's (and Kierkegaard's) views of personal sovereignty are such that political activity must inevitably be regarded as another form of the dreaded abstraction.* Reform is likely to become ideological extortion at worst and unthinking abstractionism at best. Political reform, like the objective-empirical method, can only add to the malaise. Percy's argument against politics is explicitly voiced in *The Last Gentleman* in Sutter's bitter dialogue with himself in his journal. Like Kierkegaard's, Sutter's cynicism about politics is matched only by his hostility toward established religion. The combination of the two,

politics and religion, in America has resulted in God having over-
stayed his welcome and taken "up with the wrong people." Politicians, preachers, Southern businessmen and all other forms of the
New Adam "are going to remake the world and go into space and they
couldn't care less whether you and God approve and sprinkle holy
water on them. They'll even let you sprinkle holy water on them and
they'll even like you because they'll know it makes no difference any
more. All you will succeed in doing is cancelling yourself. At least
have the courage of your revolt" (*LG*, pp. 308–309). The seductive
possibilities of revolt to which Sutter refers (and to which I shall
return) are considerably diluted by the knowledge that his form of it
came when he "turned [his] back on the bastards and went into the
desert,"—much as the Christ goes into exile.

The complete political and social implications of Binx Bolling's
malaise and Sutter's bitterness are manifested in *Love in the Ruins*
when Thomas More chastises the "Christ-haunted," "Christ-forgetting America," the "death-dealing" America which was given Israel,
Greece, science and art, the new world—indeed, lordship of the earth.

> And all you had to do was pass one little test, which was surely child's
> play for you because you had already passed the big one. One little test:
> Here's a helpless man in Africa, all you have to do is not violate him. That's
> all.
> One little test: You flunk! (*LR*, p. 57)

So while *Love in the Ruins* chides our love affair with political
pluralism; attacks the politics of the sixties and its abstractionist slo-
gans of peace, brotherhood and Great Societies; and inveighs against
mass society and its malaise; it is America, Christ and race that bring
us tragedy.

Percy, the Southern existentialist Catholic (with a Greek-Roman
heritage) is surely angry with the impotence and disorder of the
sixties. He is cynical about politics and horrified by mass urban society. Finally, he views the New Israel's (America's) handling of the
racial problem as tragic in nature. At the core of all of these critiques of
politics is the view, assumed from Kierkegaard, that "The new development in our age cannot be political for politics is a dialectical
relation between the individual and the community in the *representa-*

tive individual; but in our times the individual is in the process of becoming far too reflective to be able to be satisfied with merely being *represented.*"[4]

In a word, *politics is an abstraction, fundamentally incompatible with the searchings of a sovereign wayfarer.* Therein lies the dilemma and the shortcoming of Percy's "political philosophy." The critique of Percy which follows is, I believe, an accurate if harsh one. I would recall Kierkegaard's deathbed conversation with Pastor Boisen. The pastor objected that Kierkegaard's attack upon Christendom "did not correspond with reality, it was more severe." Kierkegaard answered, "So it must be; otherwise it does not help."

The political relationship is primordial. It involves more than ideology and protest movements, more than elections and legislatures, more than a philosophy of order. Politics is an inevitable, an inherent part of being-in-the-world. As Martin Buber puts it, "the basic structure of otherness, in many ways uncanny but never quite unholy or incapable of being hallowed, in which I and others who meet me in my life are inwoven, is the body politic"[5] Thus the political relationship is a part of the dialectical unfolding of consciousness of the self as self and consciousness of "otherness."

When Kierkegaard and Percy turn away from the horrors of malformation that this dialectical relationship has taken in the modern era, they turn away not only from the distortion of politics but from the genus, the body politic which has the potential of "men turning to one another in the context of creation. The false formations distort but they cannot eliminate the eternal origin"[6] This refusal to fully consider the dialectical possibilities of being-in-the-world as being-a-self and being-with-others reveals itself in Percy's failure to grapple with similar dialectical tensions in his stances as diagnostician, existential phenomenologist and Christian thinker.

As a diagnostician, Percy has disavowed the role of therapist. He writes in what he calls the Christian context, "having cast his lot with a discredited Christendom and having inherited a defunct vocabulary" (*MB*, p. 118). Yet he believes the novelist lacks authority to preach the "good news."[7] He writes the apocalyptic novel without announcing the second coming. The novelist is the diagnostician but not the therapist because "Whether or not the catastrophe actually befalls us, or is deserved—whether reconciliation and renewal may yet take place—is not for the novelist to say" (*MB*, p. 118). He does not speak with authority because in the Christian sense he lacks the credentials of the apostolic newsbearer whose authority is the "gravity of his message" and whose acceptance is dependent upon our faith.

Despite his insistence on being diagnostician and not therapist, Percy is both. The novel, especially the phenomenological novel, is therapy itself, aside from any message it may or may not contain. It can impart the very great knowledge that "At least we know that we are lost to ourselves" (*MB*, p. 93). That is no small achievement since as Percy insists on numerous occasions, to be a castaway and to pretend one is not is despair. Like Camus, Percy believes that those who write the so-called literature of alienation (or for that matter any other form of phenomenological novel) can use the language skillfully to name being and achieve an aesthetic victory of sorts. Percy never seems to anguish over the fact that the novel is a poor substitute for experience, an aesthetic victory and not an ethical or existential one.

A more serious difficulty inherent in this distinction between diagnosis and therapy is the failure to recognize the dialectical relationship between the two. While naming the malaise is no small victory, naming is clearly not sufficient. A diagnosis contains certain criteria for looking at the world—Percy's tends to ignore the world of otherness or attends only to its "distorted face." But a diagnosis also points the way toward therapy, and a distorted diagnosis will lead to a distorted therapy. In making a diagnosis one must be cognizant of the "therapies" inherent in that diagnosis. An explicit formulation of such therapies, a raising of "theoretical self-consciousness"[8] can only lead to greater awareness of the ground upon which one's political views are resting. In this sense Percy's novels focus not on the "how" of being-in-the-world but on the "fate" of living as a single one in modern society. It is precisely because he does not consciously consider the therapeutic that his diagnosis falls short. A therapy is there, whether consciously or unconsciously perpetrated.

Percy's vision of individual authenticity or salvation or escape from the malaise is so imbued with the notion of the "sovereign pilgrim" and so highly critical of abstract solutions that attempts at political or social reform, institutional or revolutionary, seem by comparison to be gnostic. Perhaps this is why he casts about, using Kierkegaard, for forms of escape from everydayness that are superficially apolitical. Ordeal, rotation and repetition are all devices his characters (and Kierkegaard's) use to combat everydayness.

Ordeal clears the air of boredom and provides the distraction, the insecurity, even the threat that makes life interesting. In this sense, *Love in the Ruins* is a novel of ordeal. But ultimately, ordeal can never be an authentic and viable source of either political community or individual sovereignty. The effectiveness of it in making us feel less alienated and more alive is testimony to our state of estrangement and little more.

Rotation is still another device for combating the malaise by taking a situation and absorbing the experience of it as one's own. By accident or by design a diversion may be created, a dialectical moment which will recover the "ordinary thing." Of course it is not the technique that is important but the consciousness necessary to decide to try a rotation or to take advantage of the accidental discovery. Where the decision comes from, Percy does not tell us. The object is to regain the lost sovereignty of the individual; and like the ordeal, the rotation cannot accomplish that task for anything other than the moment. What it does signal, however, is a state of what Percy often calls "waiting, watching and listening," the capacity for the unexpected. This is a tricky business; too much preparation for the unexpected will only result in the mundane. What Percy is getting at, I suspect, is an openness to the news (the Good News as far as he is concerned). But rotation itself is a tactic, a diversionary device. It may be a manifestation of a deeper consciousness and therefore have a more significant importance to social existence. But it need not be.

Repetition has its dual nature also. It can be the continued repetitive savoring of an event or experience such as Binx Bolling's listening to the same radio programs; or it can be a return, an existential return in time in search of self, a "zone-crossing," such as Will Barrett attempts in his travels and most importantly in confronting his father's suicide. In the former sense repetition is like rotation and ordeal, a superficial momentary aesthetic device. In the latter sense it is a significant event, an announcement of a state of consciousness which can give rise not only to an authentic sovereign existence but also to the possibility of community with others, to intersubjectivity, if the search can somewhere culminate in acceptance of self and others.

Percy's therapy, the key to his social and political thought, is ultimately grounded in a change in consciousness. Because of its importance, I choose to consider it outside the circumscription of ordeal, rotation and repetition. It is the "struggle" for acceptance, for grace.[9] But the difficulties of the diagnostician caused by a failure to recognize the world of politics as primordial are made even more manifest when the therapy is made explicit. Percy's dilemma remains.

As an existential phenomenologist Percy has to contend with the relationship between experience and consciousness without regressing into a Cartesian dualism of subject and object. The problem is, quite simply, how to recover the concrete, the personal aspect of existence without positing a philosophy of incarnation, or as Paul Ricoeur puts it, how to steer a path between the "carnal and the mysterious."[10] Being, in such a balance, can be revealed as both concrete experience and ontological mystery. And, as argued above, being as concrete experience must involve facing the dilemmas and the possibilities in the world of otherness, the world of politics. Indeed, if there is any essential thrust to the combination of existentialism and phenomenology, it is the focus on the political relation, on the problem of the self-existing-in-a-world-with-others.

As a Christian, Percy is faced with a similar dilemma. There is a dynamic tension between grace as "the Word" and grace as "the Word made Flesh." In political terms the matter can be phrased in the form of a query: Is the answer to the modern malaise a turning away from the world in an introspective search for personal sovereignty? Or is it the attempt to transform the culture and rebuild the kingdom—an attempt at participating in the laborious tasks of rebellion, reconciliation and renewal? Percy's writings, closely aligned as they are with Kierkegaard, suggest the former of these two alternatives. I shall argue that the change in consciousness Percy depicts in his characters, rooted as it is in the Christian notion of Grace, demands acceptance of both contrary alternatives.

"Man in his pure nature," wrote Paul Tillich, "is not only the image of God; he has also the power of communion with God and therefore of righteousness toward other creatures and himself. With the fall this power has been lost. Man is separated from God and he has no freedom of return."[11] Thus the fundamentally separated state in which we live is our state of estrangement from ourselves, each other and God or Being. It is our existence. To paraphrase Tillich, before sin can be an act it is a state of existence, namely separation. Grace is reconciliation, the "infusion of love" which gives power to overcome estrangement.[12] It is precisely this kind of estrangement and this kind of reconciliation which Percy's characters experience.

Binx Bolling, after Aunt Emily lectures him on his failure to live up to "expectations," recognizes the possibility of the search anew, accepts his despair and Kate's and makes a commitment to her and the absurdity of their marriage. Will Barrett at the end of *The Last Gentleman* utters the confession of acceptance to Sutter, "Dr. Vaught, I need you. I, Will Barrett— . . . need you" (*LG*, p. 409). And Max Gottlieb's diagnosis in *Love in the Ruins* that "Dr. More is having some troublesome mood swings—don't we all . . ." (*LR*, p. 110) is an act of acceptance and recognition of the commonality of suffering. It is grace, and it is the beginning of the political community because it recognizes the bonds of human suffering. In all three instances there is some intersubjectivity, a subtle, quiet acceptance of self and others. Binx Bolling, Will Barrett and Dr. More exhibit the faith necessary to enter into some kind of tentative relationship with another. The faith is painful, the change in consciousness subtle compared to the "willed idealism" of an Aunt Emily or an Art Immelmann.[13]

But if one looks carefully at the "reconciled" one sees that outwardly there is little formal change. Binx marries Kate, goes to medical school and tends to his kin. Will Barrett will marry Kitty and operate his father-in-law's Chevrolet agency; and Dr. More ends up where he began, in bed with Early Times whiskey and his new wife, Ellen. The unavoidable conclusion is that the most significant change that occurs in these pilgrims' progress is one of consciousness, that "the index to authenticity is not in actions but in consciousness."[14] There is, to be fair to Percy, a tentative outreach into the arena of what he and Gabriel Marcel call intersubjectivity, in other words the beginnings of relationships that may be predicated on love of the other as the "Thou" as opposed to the "it." It may be that in these "consciousness" novels Percy is preparing the way for a new and perhaps more socially based emphasis on love and the politics of community building. He has indicated that the three novels are intended as a gloss on Kierkegaard and that he will not write another like them.[15] (Unfortunately, his fourth novel, *Lancelot*, is a continuation of the theme of hyperindividualistic consciousness.) But Kierkegaard was interested in becoming the "single one" who would not be absorbed by the absolute. Waiting, watching and listening on the bayou is not sufficient; and the desire to do so arises from a fundamental misunderstanding of or a reluctance to pursue the implications of a politics of grace.

The Pauline and Augustinian views of grace stress the divine intervention of mercy into human affairs. Both views are often opposed to the law: "if you are led by the Spirit you are not under the law" (Galatians 5:18 RSV). There are similarities in the dualism and the immanent-transcendent dichotomy so important in the political philosophy of Eric Voegelin and his followers. In their criticism of politics, which is not unlike Percy's, those who insist on such a dichotomy usually point to the failure of modern gnostic movements that attempt to overcome the gulf between immanence and transcendence by the creation of a new man, or a new order of being which will be a marked improvement over the previous order. More often than not, the insistence on such a dichotomy and the subsequent critique of any type of immanent utopian thinking regards change in human nature or character as simply not possible. This is particularly noteworthy, as we have seen, in Percy's characters. Salvation, the making whole of the person, is primarily a matter of consciousness. But the emphasis by Percy on *consciousness at the expense of experience*, on grace as "Word" and not as "Word made Flesh" does a grave injustice to Christianity as well as to the notion of grace. One of the fundamental traits of Christianity is the emphasis on the capacity for change, the potentiality for the new creation, the new being, the belief that one can say with the prophet, "Behold I am doing a new thing" (Isaiah 43: 18–19, RSV).

The view of grace which negates the possibility of change, ironically and quite contradictorily, does not allow the personal or communal response of the human being to grace through freedom and will. "Theologically speaking, Spirit, love, and grace are one and the same reality in different aspects. Spirit is the creative power, love is its creation, grace is the *effective* presence of love in man."[16] The paradox of grace is its immanent *and* transcendent character. Being is both transcendent and immanent. Certainly Being is open to us through grace; but being is immanent in us, entrusted to us as will. That is why Being as authentic doing of the truth involves courage and the "risk of creation."[17] That is why Kierkegaard, who may not have perceived the social implications of grace, quite correctly used the dramatic phrase "leap of faith" as a description of what it takes to "risk creation" and "do the truth." *Percy's characters do not leap. They take small, unsure, timid steps toward half-realized pilgrimages.*

Ironically a profoundly religious unbeliever, Albert Camus, posits a more authentic view of the politics of grace in one of his final works, a short story entitled "The Growing Stone."[18] D'Arrast, a French civil engineer in Camus's story, comes to a Brazilian village to direct the construction of a dam. He arrives during a religious festival and is made welcome but significantly is not comfortable enough to feel he can fully participate in that joyous occasion. D'Arrast befriends a recently shipwrecked ship's cook who prayed to the Virgin Mary to be spared drowning, absurdly promising in return to carry a stone on his head from his home to the village church. Exhausted from a night of drink and dance and suffering from the day's intense heat, the cook struggles to fulfill his vow. But the stone weighs too painfully on his head, and he collapses in defeat. D'Arrast instinctively (because he does not share the cook's belief in the deity) loads the stone on his own shoulders and carries it through the village not to the church but to the cook's hut, where he kicks open the door and hurls it onto the fire in the center of the room. "And there, straightening up until he was suddenly enormous, drinking in with desperate gulps the familiar smell of poverty and ashes, he felt rising within him a surge of obscure and panting joy that he was powerless to name."[19]

That is grace in its immanent and transcendent aspects. It is intuitive in nature, felt; but it is community through action. As Dr. Rieux in *The Plague* puts it, one cannot cure and know at the same time; the task therefore is to cure. D'Arrast standing in the darkness acclaims, "once again, a fresh beginning in life," and is invited by the cook's brother to "sit down with us."[20] The politics of grace in Camus involves a revolt against suffering and death which continues in spite of the knowledge that it can never be complete; that total justice is a dream. It is a revolt that must be lucid and faithful to the human condition, to the sensual not the abstract aspects of politics. The shared experience of humankind can be the empirical base from which radical change can emerge. It can be something both more and less than hellish totalitarianism or bureaucratic abstractionism. That experience is what Plato called *pathos*. It is what happens to us, what we suffer, what touches our existential core. "The community of pathos is the basis of communication. Behind the hardened, intellectually supported attitudes which separate men, lie the *pathemata* which bind them together. However false and grotesque the intellectual position may be, the pathos at the core has the truth of an immediate experience. If one can penetrate to this core and reawaken in a man the awareness of his *conditio humana*, communication in the existential sense becomes possible."[21]

Pathos, the common sufferings of human kind, can be linked with the notion of "care"and given ontological status. A society or individual without care is in a condition of a-pathos, apathy. [22] Conversely the "care structure" of an individual or a society, the way he, she or it "cares" for its poor, hungry and sick is an indication of how well it has become aware of its *conditio humana*. But it is not just the *pathemata* that binds humans together; it is the rebellion against agony. Thus, existential pathos is both the beginning of rebellion and the continuation of authentic political existence. That rebellion need not be destructive if it is possessed of a "saving grace," namely recognition of the fact that it must involve a love, which as Tillich puts it, has "the courage to judge the particular without subjecting it to an abstract norm, a courage which can do justice to the norm."[23] Courage here, as with care in Heidegger's thought, becomes an ontological act, the affirmation of being in spite of non-being.

The politics of grace begins with a recognition of the essential givenness of the world (the world-as-self and the world-as-others) and proceeds to the existential task of how to live in that world. The Christian view of how to exist in the world must involve "building the Kingdom," and that requires participation in rebellion, reconciliation and renewal: rebellion against the agony of human suffering; reconciliation with oneself and with others; and a renewal into the creative new being. Walker Percy's novels portray us as fated individuals in a world of malaise. Because there is little recognition in them of the priority of social existence, there is little indication that the rebellion of his characters is social at all. Indeed, in *Love in the Ruins* he scoffs at such resistance. In *Lancelot* a resistance occurs, but it is destructively maniacal and asocial in form. Hence the reconciliation that Binx Bolling, Will Barrett, Dr. More and Lancelot participate in is incomplete; their renewal is partial.

By refusing to recognize the dialectical tension between grace as "the Word" and grace as "the Word made flesh" Percy has essentially taken the Kierkegaardian road toward viewing being-in-the-world as Promethean and Orphic choices characterized by either/or alternatives. Either we destroy the reality we face in order to recover ourselves or ignore the reality we face in order to recover ourselves. The logical conclusion of this either/or stance is reached in Lancelot who longs for a new order based upon "stern rectitude" and "marked by the violence which will attend its breach" (*L*, p. 158). The reality Lancelot perceives, our world as Sodom, is so distorted, so lacking in grace, that his apocalyptic "solution" of fire and violence lacks social significance as well as moral authority.

An authentic politics of grace begins with the assumption that we shall have politics whether we like it or not. We are thrust into the necessity of choosing whether we shall have a politics of abstraction or one of sensual concern. Rebellion in this context must take place in immanent time, in the realm of experience, or the result will likely be some form of mystic nihilism. But it must also accept the fact that to ignore the transcendent character of existence, to insist upon nothing but history or experience, will cause it to disintegrate into metaphysical disillusionment.[24] The Prometheus/Orpheus alternatives are transformed into a dialectic.

Camus's "The Growing Stone" is included in a volume entitled *Exile and the Kingdom*. Camus recognizes, like Percy, that we are all outcasts in the modern era; but he insists that our rebellion against the *form* that politics has taken must lead to a renewed attempt at building the community of grace. Unlike Sutter the paradoxical Galilean returns from his exile in the wilderness and announces that he is going to "bind up hearts that are broken" and "proclaim liberty to captives" and "freedom to those in prison."[25] If exile is the permanent stance of the Christian, the attempt to build the kingdom must be also. That attempt must consider the kingdom in both its immanent presence and its future potentiality. Dr. More knows of no such attempt; Binx Bolling is overcome by it; Sutter and Will Barrett are inconclusive in their search for it; and Lancelot pursues a demented form of it.

Another quite different image of exile and kingdom for the post-modern world is Job, one who affirms the given of existence and at the same time contends with it. As Maurice Friedman argues, "in the modern Job the problematic becomes a ground, the paradox of the person a stance, exile and rebellion a way."[26] There is no doubt as to the appropriateness of the latter typology for a politics built upon the foundations of grace, just as there is no doubt that Walker Percy has given us a vivid and compelling image of exile in our modern era. We must continue, however, to wait, watch and listen for a more authentic naming of rebellion.

NOTES

I must thank James Bolner, Candace Pickering, David Lange and Walter Mays for critically reviewing earlier versions of this essay and express my gratitude to Josephine Scurria for her assistance in its final preparation.

[1]*Steppenwolf*, trans. Basil Creighton (New York: Holt, Rinehart and Winston, Inc., 1929), pp. 22–23.

[2]Friedrich Nietzsche, *The Gay Science* in *The Portable Nietzsche*, trans. and ed. Walter Kaufmann (New York: Viking Press, Inc., 1969), pp. 95–96.

[3]*The Sovereign Wayfarer* (Baton Rouge: Louisiana State Univ. Press, 1967), pp. 21–34.

[4]Søren Kierkegaard, *The Journals of Søren Kierkegaard*, ed. and trans. Alexander Dru (London: Oxford Univ. Press, 1938), p. 151.

[5]*Between Man and Man* (New York: The Macmillan Co., 1965), p. 61.

[6]Ibid., p. 60.

[7]John Carr, "An Interview with Walker Percy," *The Georgia Review*, 25 (Fall 1971), 326.

[8]See William Connolly's discussion of this phenomenon and its relevance to modern social science in "Theoretical Self-Consciousness," *Polity*, 6 (Fall 1973), 5–35.

[9]I use the word *struggle* consciously since the courage to accept acceptance is not usually an event-in-time but a process. In *The Sovereign Wayfarer* Martin Luschei suggests that the wit and humor of *Love in the Ruins* provides another form of grace, comic therapy. Humor does have the capacity to heal, but the humor of *Love in the Ruins* too frequently degenerates into sarcasm. It resembles Nietzschean *ressentiment*, which is the opposite of grace. For an excellent discussion of the theme of grace and humor, see John Zeugner, "Walker Percy and Gabriel Marcel: The Castaway and the Wayfarer," *Mississippi Quarterly*, 28 (Winter 1974–75), 21–53.

[10]"Existential Phenomenology," in *Phenomenology and Existentialism*, ed. Richard M. Zaner and Don Ihde (New York: G. P. Putnam's Sons, Capricorn Books, 1973), p. 94.

[11]*Systematic Theology* (Chicago: The University of Chicago Press, 1967), I, 258. See also Paul Tillich, "You are Accepted," in *The Shaking of the Foundations* (New York: Charles Scribner's Sons, 1948).

[12]Paul Tillich, *Systematic Theology* (Chicago: The University of Chicago Press, 1967), II, 49.

[13]See Jim Van Cleave, "Versions of Percy," *The Southern Review*, 6 (October 1970), 990–1010 for an excellent discussion of "willed idealism" in *The Moviegoer*.

[14]Ibid., p. 1008.

[15]Martin Luschei, *The Sovereign Wayfarer* notes in this regard: "He [Percy] told me this and said he would never write another like them," p. 241.

[16]Paul Tillich, *Systematic Theology* (Chicago: The University of Chicago Press, 1967), III, 274. Italics are mine.

[17]This phrase and with it the development of the paradox of grace owes a great debt to the writings of John Macquarrie, *Principles of Christian Theology* (New York: Charles Scribner's Sons, 1966); Dietrich Bonhoeffer, *The Cost of Discipleship* (New York: The Macmillan Company, 1963); and of course the *Systematic Theology* of Paul Tillich.

[18]*The Fall* and *Exile and the Kingdom*, trans. Justin O'Brien (New York: Random House, Inc., The Modern Library, 1958), pp. 307–361. See also Fred H. Willhoite, Jr., *Beyond Nihilism: Albert Camus' Contribution to Political Thought* (Baton Rouge: Louisiana State Univ. Press, 1968).

[19]Camus, "The Growing Stone," p. 360.

[20]Ibid., pp. 360–61.

[21]Eric Voegelin, *Plato and Aristotle* (Baton Rouge: Louisiana State Univ. Press, 1957), pp. 29–30.

[22]See Rollo May's excellent discussion of this and Heidegger's concept of *sorge* or "care" in *Love and Will* (New York: W. W. Norton and Company, Inc., 1969).

[23]Tillich, *Systematic Theology*, III, 274.

[24]Utopian thinking is very similar in its paradoxical character. An excellent discussion of the positive, negative and transcendent aspects of utopia which I have relied upon in developing a theory of grace and politics is Paul Tillich, "Critique and Justification of Utopia," *Utopias and Utopian Thought*, ed. Frank E. Manuel (Boston: Beacon Press, 1967), pp. 296–309.

[25]See Isaiah 61:1 and Luke 4:14–19, *The Jerusalem Bible*. For an excellent discussion of the role of the exiled hero who returns to renew the community see Joseph Campbell, *The Hero With a Thousand Faces* (New York: Pantheon Books, 1949).

[26]*The Problematic Rebel*, revised edition (Chicago: The University of Chicago Press, 1970), p. 491.

A Walker Percy Bibliography

JOE WEIXLMANN and DANIEL H. GANN

Building on the admirable pioneering work of Scott Byrd and John F. Zeugner ("Walker Percy: A Checklist," *Bulletin of Bibliography*, 30, No. 1 [1973], 16–17, 44), we have attempted to compile a thorough primary and secondary Percy bibliography. Space limitations imposed by *The Southern Quarterly* required some minor exclusions: reprints, mere "mentions," and the biographical blurbs one finds in anthologies, *Who's Who* volumes, and the like. These (hopefully inconsequential) items excepted, the bibliography is exhaustive.

Section I of this four-part checklist offers chronological listings of Percy's books and the reviews of them. Section II, also chronological, notes Percy's shorter publications—including those essays collected in his 1975 book *The Message in the Bottle*, which are identified by the annotation "In *MB*." Percy's interviews and other printed remarks are given chronological treatment in Section III. Section IV, devoted to the criticism of Percy's work, is arranged alphabetically by author within seven subsections: the critiques of each of the five books, general studies, and dissertations and theses. An asterisk (*) precedes the one item we have been unable to verify.

The publication, early in 1979, of Robert Coles's *Walker Percy: An American Search*; the appearance of the Louisiana State University Press's newly released collection of critical essays, *The Art of Walker Percy: Stratagems for Being* (which is referred to in this checklist by its editor's surname, Broughton); and the issuance of this special number of *The Southern Quarterly*—coupled with the hundreds of critiques documented in this bibliography—evidence Percy's conspicuous presence on the American literary scene.

I. BOOKS, WITH REVIEWS

The Moviegoer. New York: Alfred A. Knopf, 1961.

(unsigned.) *Virginia Kirkus' Service*, 29 (1 Apr. 1961), 339–40.
McCleary, William. *Library Journal*, 86 (15 May 1961), 1905.
(unsigned.) "Two True Sounds from Dixie." *Time*, 77 (19 May 1961), 105.
Poore, Charles. "Books of The Times." *The New York Times*, 27 May 1961, p. 21.

Massie, Robert. "Double Features Were His Refuge." *The New York Times Book Review*, 28 May 1961, p. 30.

Kennebeck, Edwin. "The Search." *The Commonweal*, 74 (2 June 1961), 260–62.

Knickerbocker, Paine. "A Provocative First Novel—And a New Civil War Narrative." *San Francisco Sunday Chronicle This World*, 4 June 1961, p. 30.

Cummings, Robert J. *Best Sellers*, 21 (15 June 1961), 122.

Gardiner, Harold C. *America*, 105 (17 June 1961), 448.

McLaughlin, Richard. *Springfield* (MA) *Republican*, 25 June 1961, p. 14C.

(unsigned.) *The Booklist and Subscription Books Bulletin*, 57 (1 July 1961), 664.

(unsigned.) *The New Yorker*, 37 (22 July 1961), 78–79.

Saxton, Mark. "Shadows on a Screen, More Real Than Life." *New York Herald Tribune Books*, 30 July 1961, p. 6.

Cook, Bruce A. *The Critic*, 20 (Sept. 1961), 44.

Cheney, Brainard. "To Restore a Fragmented Image." *The Sewanee Review*, 69 (Autumn 1961), 691–700.

McC[udden], J[ohn]. "Sermons and a Searcher." *Perspectives* (Notre Dame, IN), 7 (Mar.-Apr. 1962), 56–57.

Davis, Douglas M. "A Southerner's 'The Moviegoer' and His Perplexing Prize." *The National Observer*, 29 Apr. 1962, p. 21.

Hyman, Stanley Edgar. "Moviegoing and Other Intimacies." *The New Leader*, 45 (30 Apr. 1962), 23–24.

(unsigned.) In *Masterplots 1962 Annual*. Ed. Frank N. Magill and Dayton Kohler. New York: Salem Press, 1962. Pp. 212–15.

(unsigned.) "Self-Sacrifice." *The* (London) *Times Literary Supplement*, 29 Mar. 1963, p. 221.

Taubman, Robert. "Feeling Better." *New Statesman*, 65 (12 Apr. 1963), 527.

Bradbury, Malcolm. "New Fiction." *Punch*, 244 (17 Apr. 1963), 573–74.

Daniel, John. "Fatality and Futility." *The Spectator*, No. 7036 (3 May 1963), pp. 572–73.

Igoe, W. J. "More Than One America." *The Tablet*, 217 (11 May 1963), 513–14.

Hoggard, James. "Death of the Vicarious." *Southwest Review*, 49 (Autumn 1964), 366–74.

Britton, Anne. *Books and Bookmen*, 11 (Mar. 1966), 79.

(unsigned.) "Paperbacks." *The* (London) *Observer*, 17 Apr. 1966, p. 22.

Fleischer, Leonore. *Publishers' Weekly*, 192 (16 Oct. 1967), 59.

Coles, Robert. *The American Scholar*, 41 (Summer 1972), 480.

Ford, Richard. "Walker Percy: Not Just Whistling Dixie." *National Review*, 29 (13 May 1977), 558, 560–64. [p. 558]

Iyer, Pico. "A Sad Tidiness: Walker Percy and the South." *London Magazine*, NS 18 (Apr. 1978), 62–66.

S[hoemaker], D[onna]. "Books of Walker Percy." *The Chronicle (of Higher Education) Review*, 5 Mar. 1979, p. R11.

The Last Gentleman. New York: Farrar, Straus and Giroux, 1966.

(unsigned.) *The Virginia Kirkus Service*, 34 (15 Apr. 1966), 444.

Kitching, Jessie. *Publishers' Weekly*, 189 (9 May 1966), 76.

Morgan, Barry. *Delta Review*, 3 (May-June 1966), 39.

Pine, John C. *Library Journal*, 91 (1 June 1966), 2877.

Douglas, Ellen. *Delta Democrat-Times* (Greenville, MS), 7 June 1966, p. 3.

DeMott, Benjamin. "The Good and the True." *Book Week*, 3 (12 June 1966), 2, 9.

Davis, Douglas M. "From Mr. Percy, A Temptation Play for Folk-Rock Age." *The National Observer*, 13 June 1966, p. 22.

Poore, Charles. "A Candide in a Brooks Brothers Suit." *The New York Times*, 16 June 1966, p. 45.

(unsigned.) "Guidebook for Lost Pilgrims." *Time*, 87 (17 June 1966), 104.

Grumbach, Doris. *America*, 114 (18 June 1966), 858.

Hicks, Granville. "One of the Roaming Kind." *Saturday Review*, 49 (18 June 1966), 29–30.

Tracy, Honor. "Humidification Engineer." *The New Republic*, 154 (18 June 1966), 27–28.

Rosenthal, Raymond. "The Ceremony of Innocence." *The New Leader*, 49 (20 June 1966), 22–23.

(unsigned.) "In the Southern Grain." *Newsweek*, 67 (20 June 1966), 106–108.

Casey, Florence. "Coming in from the Cold." *The Christian Science Monitor*, 23 June 1966, p. 7.

Goodman, Walter. "An Elegant Quest for Ordinariness." *Life*, 60 (24 June 1966), 20.

Buitenhuis, Peter. "A Watcher, a Listener, a Wanderer." *The New York Times Book Review*, 26 June 1966, p. 5.

Donadio, Stephen. "America, America." *Partisan Review*, 33 (Summer 1966), 448–52. [pp. 451–52]

Christopher, Michael. *U.S. Catholic*, 32 (July 1966), 47–48.

Phillips, Robert. "Southern Chronicle." *The North American Review*, NS 3 (July 1966), 37–38.

Dollen, Charles. *Best Sellers*, 26 (1 July 1966), 133.

Butcher, Fanny. "Tale with a Picaresque Quality." *Chicago Tribune Books Today*, 24 July 1966, p. 10.

Wain, John. "The Insulted and the Injured." *The New York Review of Books*, 7 (28 July 1966), 22–24. [pp. 23–24]

Knipp, Thomas. *The Sign*, 46 (Aug. 1966), 59–60.

Oates, Joyce Carol. "Gentleman without a Past." *The Nation*, 203 (8 Aug. 1966), 129–30.

Wilkie, Brian. *Commonweal*, 84 (19 Aug. 1966), 537–39.

Crews, Frederick C. "The Hero as 'Case.'" *Commentary*, 42 (Sept. 1966), 100–102.

(unsigned.) *Choice*, 3 (Sept. 1966), 522.

(unsigned.) *The Booklist and Subscription Books Bulletin*, 63 (1 Sept. 1966), 34.

Morse, J. Mitchell. "Fiction Chronicle." *The Hudson Review*, 19 (Autumn 1966), 507–14. [pp. 509–10]

Trachtenberg, Stanley. "Beyond Initiation: Some Recent Novels." *The Yale Review*, 56 (Autumn 1966), 131–38. [pp. 137–38] (unsigned.) *The Virginia Quarterly Review*, 42 (Autumn 1966), cxxxiii, cxxxvi.

Johnson, Lucy. "Percy and Amis." *The Progressive*, 30 (Oct. 1966), 49–50.

Sheed, Wilfrid. "Ravening Particles of Anxiety." *The Critic*, 25 (Oct.-Nov. 1966), 92–93.

McNaspy, C. J. *Commonweal*, 85 (2 Dec. 1966), 268–69. [p. 269]

Price, R. G. G. "New Novels." *Punch*, 252 (8 Feb. 1967), 210.

Sheed, Wilfrid. "Additions to the Galaxy." *The National Catholic Reporter*, 3 (8 Feb. 1967), 7.

Klein, Marcus. "Melted into Air." *The Reporter*, 36 (9 Feb. 1967), 61–62.

Braybrooke, Neville. "The Cruel Time." *The Spectator*, No. 7235 (24 Feb. 1967), p. 228.

Cheney, Brainard. "Secular Society as Deadly Farce." *The Sewanee Review*, 75 (Spring 1967), 345–50.

Lehan, Richard. "The American Novel: A Survey of 1966." *Wisconsin Studies in Contemporary Literature*, 8 (Summer 1967), 437–49. [pp. 439–40]

Hayes, Richard. *Commonweal*, 87 (1 Dec. 1967), 308.

(unsigned.) "The American Game of Happy Families." *The* (London) *Times Literary Supplement*, 21 Dec. 1967, p. 1233.

Pendleton, Dennis. In *Masterplots 1967 Annual*. Ed. Frank N. Magill and Dayton Kohler. New York: Salem Press, 1968. Pp. 184–86.

Fleischer, Leonore. *Publishers' Weekly*, 193 (29 Jan. 1968), 100.

Petersen, Clarence. "Paperbacks." *Book World*, 2 (10 Mar. 1968), 11.

Dickey, James. *The American Scholar*, 37 (Summer 1968), 524.

Wolfe, Peter. "Knowing the Noumenon." *Prairie Schooner*, 42 (Summer 1968), 181–85.

Coles, Robert. *The American Scholar*, 41 (Summer 1972), 480.

Ford, Richard. "Walker Percy: Not Just Whistling Dixie." *National Review*, 29 (13 May 1977), 558, 560–64. [pp. 558, 560–61]

Lee, Hermione. "Catfish Fry." *New Statesman*, 95 (3 Mar. 1978), 294–95.

S[hoemaker], D[onna]. "Books of Walker Percy." *The Chronicle (of Higher Education) Review*, 5 Mar. 1979, p. R11.

Love in the Ruins: The Adventures of a Bad Catholic at a Time Near the End of the World. New York: Farrar, Straus and Giroux, 1971.

(unsigned.) *Kirkus Reviews*, 39 (15 Mar. 1971), 319.

Bannon, Barbara A. *Publishers' Weekly*, 199 (29 Mar. 1971), 44.

(unsigned.) *Kirkus Reviews*, 39 (15 Apr. 1971), 454–55.

Wasson, Ben. "Broken with Happiness." *Delta Democrat-Times* (Greenville, MS), 25 Apr. 1971, p. 6.

Avant, John Alfred. *Library Journal*, 96 (15 May 1971), 1728–29.

Broyard, Anatole. "Apocalypses and Other Ills." *The New York Times*, 15 May 1971, p. 29.

Catinella, Joseph. *Saturday Review*, 54 (15 May 1971), 42–43.

Hill, William B. *Best Sellers*, 31 (15 May 1971), 85.

Price, Reynolds. "Walker Percy in the Ruins." *Chicago Daily News Panorama*, 15–16 May 1971, p. 7.

Douglas, Ellen. *Delta Democrat-Times* (Greenville, MS), 16 May 1971, p. 6.

Theroux, Paul. "Christian Science-Fiction." *Book World*, 5 (16 May 1971), 4.

Anderson, David C. "Mr. Percy's Positive Statement." *The Wall Street Journal*, 17 May 1971, p. 12.

Duffy, Martha. "Lapsometer Legend." *Time*, 97 (17 May 1971), 94. [Includes printed remarks by Percy]

Pettingell, Phoebe. "Walker Percy's Sci-Fi Detour." *The New Leader*, 54 (17 May 1971), 11–12.

Prescott, Peter S. "The Big Breakdown." *Newsweek*, 77 (17 May 1971), 106–107.

Davenport, Guy. "Mr. Percy's Look at Chaos, 1983." *Life*, 70 (21 May 1971), 16.

Hill, William B. *America*, 124 (22 May 1971), 548.

Yardley, Jonathan. "Stethoscope of the Spirit." *The New Republic*, 164 (22 May 1971), 25–26.

McGuane, Thomas. "This Is the Way the World Will End." *The New York Times Book Review*, 23 May 1971, pp. 7, 37.

Cook, Bruce. "To Walker Percy, Man's Prognosis Is Funny." *The National Observer*, 24 May 1971, p. 17. [Includes printed remarks by Percy]

Marsh, Pamela. "Tomorrow the World Ends." *The Christian Science Monitor*, 3 June 1971, p. 10.

(unsigned.) *The New York Times Book Review*, 6 June 1971, p. 3.

Rule, Philip C. *America*, 124 (12 June 1971), 617.

McPherson, William. "The Greening and the Crumbling." *The Washington Post*, 17 June 1971, pp. C1, C6.

(unsigned.) *The Antioch Review*, 31 (Summer 1971), 283.

(unsigned.) *The Virginia Quarterly Review*, 47 (Summer 1971), xcvi.

(unsigned.) *American Libraries*, 2 (July 1971), 762.

Pritchett, V. S. "Clowns." *The New York Review of Books*, 16 (1 July 1971), 15.

(unsigned.) *The Booklist*, 67 (1 July 1971), 895–96.

Sheed, Wilfrid. "The Good Word: Walker Percy Redivivus." *The New York Times Book Review*, 4 July 1971, p. 2.

Smith, Julian. "Elegant Paranoia." *Christian Century*, 88 (7 July 1971), 835.

Janeway, Elizabeth. " 'The End of the World Is Coming.' " *The Atlantic Monthly*, 228 (Aug. 1971), 87–90. [p. 88]

Murray, Michele. "Bad Catholic Stars in Crazy Plot." *The National Catholic Reporter*, 7 (27 Aug. 1971), 7.

Deutsch, Alfred. *Sisters Today*, 43 (Aug.-Sept. 1971), 57–58.

Cormier, Robert. *The Sign*, 51 (Sept. 1971), 48–49.

Hope, Francis. "Armageddon in the Swamps." *The* (London) *Observer*, 5 Sept. 1971, p. 27.

Sissman, L. E. "Inventions." *The New Yorker*, 47 (11 Sept. 1971), 121–22, 124–26. [pp. 121–22, 124]

Fielding, Gabriel. *The Critic*, 30 (Sept.-Oct. 1971), 69–72.

Morse, J. Mitchell. "Fiction Chronicle." *The Hudson Review*, 24 (Fall 1971), 526–40. [pp. 531–33]

(unsigned.) *Choice*, 8 (Oct. 1971), 1018.

(unsigned.) "Lapsed from Grace." *The* (London) *Times Literary Supplement*, 1 Oct. 1971, p. 1165.

Taylor, Mark. *Commonweal*, 95 (29 Oct. 1971), 118–19.

Horner, Antony. *Books and Bookmen*, 17 (Nov. 1971), 45.

(unsigned.) *Saturday Review*, 54 (27 Nov. 1971), 46.

Kiley, John. "Something Else." *Triumph*, 6 (Dec. 1971), 32–35.

MacEoin, Gary. *St. Anthony Messenger*, 79 (Dec. 1971), 55.

(unsigned.) *The New York Times Book Review*, 5 Dec. 1971, p. 83.

Prescott, Peter S. "The Year in Books: A Personal Report." *Newsweek*, 78 (27 Dec. 1971), 57, 60–61. [p. 60]

Goodwin, Stephen. "After the Faulkner." *Shenandoah*, 23 (Winter 1972), 70–77. [pp. 75–77]

Hynes, Joseph. "Percy's Reliques." *Cross Currents*, 22 (Winter 1972), 117–20, 128.

Lottman, Eileen. *Publishers' Weekly*, 201 (27 Mar. 1972), 80.

Coles, Robert. *The American Scholar*, 41 (Summer 1972), 480.

Gaillard, Dawson. *The New Orleans Review*, 2, No. 4 (1972), 379–81.

(unsigned.) "Fiction." *Best Sellers*, 32 (1 Aug. 1972), 223–24. [p. 223]

Broughton, Panthea Reid. In *Masterplots 1972 Annual*. Ed. Frank N. Magill. Englewood Cliffs, NJ: Salem Press, 1972. Pp. 205–208.

(unsigned.) *Catholic Library World*, 44 (Feb. 1973), 425.

Yardley, Jonathan. "The New Old Southern Novel." *Partisan Review*, 40, No. 2 (1973), 286–93. [p. 293]

Bradford, Melvin E. "Dr. Percy's Paradise Lost: Diagnostics in Louisiana." *The Sewanee Review*, 81 (Autumn 1973), 839–44. See also Brainard Cheney, "Correspondence," *The Sewanee Review*, 82 (Winter 1974), 194–96.

Garvey, John. "Fantastic Stories." *Commonweal*, 102 (1 Aug. 1975), 314–15. [p. 315]

Ford, Richard. "Walker Percy: Not Just Whistling Dixie." *National Review*, 29 (13 May 1977), 558, 560–64. [pp. 561–62]

Lee, Hermione. "Catfish Fry." *New Statesman*, 95 (3 Mar. 1978), 294–95.

S[hoemaker], D[onna]. "Books of Walker Percy." *The Chronicle (of Higher Education) Review*, 5 Mar. 1979, p. R11.

The Message in the Bottle: How Queer Man Is, How Queer Language Is, and What One Has to Do with the Other. New York: Farrar, Straus and Giroux, 1975.

(unsigned.) *Kirkus Reviews*, 43 (15 Apr. 1975), 497.

Johnston, Albert H. *Publishers' Weekly*, 207 (28 Apr. 1975), 42.

McMurtry, Larry. "What Language Reveals—And What It Conceals." *The Washington Post*, 19 May 1975, p. B6.

Hatcher, Burnett. *Delta Democrat-Times* (Greenville, MS), 8 June 1975, p. 31.

LeClair, Thomas. "For Walker Percy Man Is the Naming Animal." *The New York Times Book Review*, 8 June 1975, pp. 6–7.

Crain, Jane Larkin. *Saturday Review*, 2 (28 June 1975), 24.

Ciardi, John. "Why Is 20th Century Man So Sad?" *Chicago Tribune Book World*, 29 June 1975, p. 6.

Harris, Sydney J. "Language in a Very Deep Bottle." *Chicago Daily News Panorama*, 5–6 July 1975, p. 8.

Fuller, Edmund. "Travels with a First-Rate Reporter." *The Wall Street Journal*, 14 July 1975, p. 8.

Boatwright, James. "Matters of Life." *The New Republic*, 173 (19 July 1975), 28–29.

Tyler, Anne. "The Topic Is Language—With Love and Skill." *The National Observer*, 19 July 1975, p. 21.

Murray, John J. *Best Sellers*, 35 (Aug. 1975), 126–27.

Zaidman, Bernard. *Library Journal*, 100 (Aug. 1975), 1417.

Cuffe, Edwin D. " 'Chickens Have No Myths.' " *America*, 133 (16 Aug. 1975), 76–77.

McNaspy, C. J. " 'Why Does Man Feel So Sad?' " *National Catholic Reporter*, 11 (29 Aug. 1975), 7.

(unsigned.) *The Booklist*, 72 (1 Sept. 1975), 14–15.

Kenner, Hugh. "On Man the Sad Talker." *National Review*, 27 (12 Sept. 1975), 1000–1002.

Nagel, Thomas. "Sin and Significance." *The New York Review of Books*, 22 (18 Sept. 1975), 54–56.

King, Richard H. "Alienation and the Word." *The New Leader*, 58 (13 Oct. 1975), 18–19.

(unsigned.) *Choice*, 12 (Dec. 1975), 1304.

Smith, Marcus. "Walker Percy: Language Mystery." *New Orleans Courier*, 27 Nov.-3 Dec. 1975, p. 10.

Wood, Ralph. "To Be a Namer." *Christian Century*, 92 (3 Dec. 1975), 1115–16.

Appleyard, J. A. *Commonweal*, 102 (5 Dec. 1975), 597–98. [p. 597]

(unsigned.) *The New York Times Book Review*, 7 Dec. 1975, p. 70.

Michaels, Walter. *The Georgia Review*, 29 (Winter 1975), 972–75.

Broughton, Panthea Reid. "A Bottle Unopened, A Message Unread." *The Virginia Quarterly Review*, 52 (Winter 1976), 155–60.

Culler, Jonathan. "Man the Symbol-Monger." *The Yale Review*, 65 (Winter 1976), 261–66. [pp. 261–64]

Dent, Huntley. *The University of Denver Quarterly*, 10 (Winter 1976), 141–42.

Scott, Robert L. *Communication Quarterly*, 24 (Winter 1976), 51–52.

Kline, Edward A. "Words, Words, Words." *The Review of Politics*, 38 (Jan. 1976), 139–41.

Lawson, Lewis A. "Walker Percy as Martian Visitor." *The Southern Literary Journal*, 8 (Spring 1976), 102–13.

Miller, Nolan. *The Antioch Review*, 34 (Spring 1976), 369.

Roddy, Kevin. *The New Orleans Review*, 5, No. 1 (1976), 79–80.

Sorum, William R. *MH*, 60 (Spring 1976), 35.

O'Donnell, Roy. *English Journal*, 65 (May 1976), 75.

McLellan, Joseph. "Paperbacks." *The Washington Post Book World*, 16 May 1976, p. L4.

Casper, Leonard. *Thought*, 51 (June 1976), 211–12.

Arrington, Robert L. "The Mystery of Language." *The Sewanee Review*, 84 (Fall 1976), cxxvii–cxxx.

Borgman, Paul C. *Christian Scholar's Review*, 6 (1976), 272–73.

Kirby, Martin. "Neither Far Out Nor in Deep." *The Carleton Miscellany*, 16 (Fall-Winter 1976–77), 209–14.

Gaston, Paul L. *Journal of Modern Literature*, 5, No. 4 (1976), 611–13.

Neilson, Keith. In *Masterplots 1976 Annual*. Ed. Frank N. Magill. Englewood Cliffs, NJ: Salem Press, 1977. Pp. 221–24.

Bigger, Charles P. "Logos and Epiphany: Walker Percy's Theology of Language." *The Southern Review*, NS 13 (Jan. 1977), 196–206.

S[hoemaker], D[onna]. "Books of Walker Percy." *The Chronicle (of Higher Education) Review*, 5 Mar. 1979, p. R11.

Lancelot. New York: Farrar, Straus and Giroux, 1977.

(unsigned.) *Kirkus Reviews*, 45 (1 Jan. 1977), 16.

Bannon, Barbara A. *Publishers' Weekly*, 211 (10 Jan. 1977), 66.

Oates, Joyce Carol. *The New Republic*, 176 (5 Feb. 1977), 32–34.

(unsigned.) *The Booklist*, 73 (15 Feb. 1977), 879.

Lehmann-Haupt, Christopher. "Camelot Lost." *The New York Times*, 17 Feb. 1977, p. 37.

Gardner, John. "The Quest for the Philosophical Novel." *The New York Times Book Review*, 20 Feb. 1977, pp. 1, 16, 20.

Hatcher, Burnett. "Another of Percy's Lonely Men." *Delta Democrat-Times* (Greenville, MS), 20 Feb. 1977, p. 37.

Goldgar, Harry. "Percy Addresses Himself to a Southern Question." *The* (New Orleans) *Times-Picayune*, 27 Feb. 1977, Sec. 3, p. 6.

Price, Reynolds. "God and Man in Louisiana." *The Washington Post Book World*, 27 Feb. 1977, pp. E7, E10.

Yardley, Jonathan. "Percy: 'I Will Not Tolerate This Age.' " *Miami Herald*, 27 Feb. 1977, p. E7.

Yount, John. "Walker Percy's Funhouse Mirror: More True Than Distorted." *Chicago Tribune Book World*, 27 Feb. 1977, p. 1.

Prescott, Peter S. "Unholy Knight." *Newsweek*, 89 (28 Feb. 1977), 73–74.

Sheed, Wilfrid. *Book-of-the-Month Club News*, Mar. 1977, pp. 1–3.

Todd, Richard. "Lead Us into Temptation, Deliver Us Evil." *The Atlantic Monthly*, 239 (Mar. 1977), 113–15.

Wiehe, Janet. *Library Journal*, 102 (1 Mar. 1977), 633.

Guidry, Frederick H. "Walker Percy's 'Lancelot.' " *The Christian Science Monitor*, 2 Mar. 1977, p. 23.

Gray, Paul. "Questing after an Unholy Grail." *Time*, 109 (7 Mar. 1977), 86–87.

Cuffe, E. D. *America*, 136 (12 Mar. 1977), 220–21.

Foote, Bud. "A New Lancelot Seeks His Knighthood." *The National Observer*, 12 Mar. 1977, p. 19.

Kendall, Elaine. "The Degradation of Lancelot in an Uncourtly Age." *The Los Angeles Times Book Review*, 13 Mar. 1977, p. 6.

Fuller, Edmund. "A Cutting Satire on Modern Life." *The Wall Street Journal*, 17 Mar. 1977, p. 18.

Wolff, Geoffrey. "The Hurricane or the Hurricane Machine." *New Times*, 8 (18 Mar. 1977), 64, 67–68.

Cook, Bruce. "The Last Man in America Who Believes in Love." *Saturday Review*, 4 (19 Mar. 1977), 28–29.

Towers, Robert. "Southern Discomfort." *The New York Review of Books*, 24 (31 Mar. 1977), 6–8.

Will, George F. "In Literature and Politics, a Quest for Values." *The Washington Post*, 31 Mar. 1977, p. A15.

Brinkmeyer, Bob. *Southern Exposure*, 5 (Spring 1977), 95–96.

Smith, Marcus. *Southern Booklore*, 1 (Spring 1977), 2.

Dubus, Andre. "Paths to Redemption." *Harper's Magazine*, 254 (Apr. 1977), 86–88.

(unsigned.) *Playboy*, 24 (Apr. 1977), 35–36.

Brown, Michael C. "Mad Southern Family Fiction of Revenge." *San Francisco Chronicle This World*, 3 Apr. 1977, p. 36.

(unsigned.) "Love & Death." *Rolling Stone*, No. 236 (7 Apr. 1977), p. 87.

Locke, Richard. "Novelists as Preachers." *The New York Times Book Review*, 17 Apr. 1977, pp. 3, 52–53.

Davis, Hope Hale. "Escape within Walls." *The New Leader*, 60 (25 Apr. 1977), 14–15.

Chesnick, Eugene. "De Comptemptu Mundi." *The Nation*, 224 (30 Apr. 1977), 533, 535–36.

T., A. *West Coast Review of Books*, 3 (May 1977), 33.

Lardner, Susan. "Miscreants." *The New Yorker*, 53 (2 May 1977), 141–44.

McNaspy, C. J. "Sick World Diagnosed." *National Catholic Reporter*, 13 (6 May 1977), 16.

Ford, Richard. "Walker Percy: Not Just Whistling Dixie." *National Review*, 29 (13 May 1977), 558, 560–64. [pp. 562–64]

Blewitt, Charles G. *Best Sellers*, 37 (June 1977), 73.

Egerton, John. "Memorable Madman." *The Progressive*, 41 (June 1977), 40–41.

(unsigned.) *Choice*, 14 (June 1977), 536.

Greeley, Andrew. "Novelists of the Madhouse." *Chicago Tribune*, 9 June 1977, Sec. 4, p. 4.

Malin, Irving. "Cross Purposes." *The Virginia Quarterly Review*, 53 (Summer 1977), 568–71.

Smith, Laurence. *The Critic*, 35 (Summer 1977), 86–89.

Wood, Ralph. "Damned in the Paradise of Sex." *Christian Century*, 94 (6–13 July 1977), 634–36.

Coser, Lewis A. "Culture & Society." *Society*, 14 (July-Aug. 1977), 85–87.

Christopher, Michael. "Days of Thorns & Roses." *U.S. Catholic*, 42 (Aug. 1977), 49–51. [pp. 49–50]

Cormier, Robert. *St. Anthony Messenger*, 85 (Sept. 1977), 45.

Glassman, Peter. "American Romances: Fiction Chronicle." *The Hudson Review*, 30 (Autumn 1977), 437–50. [pp. 443–44]

Thwaite, Anthony. "Southern Pooterism." *The* (London) *Observer*, 16 Oct. 1977, p. 37.

Barnes, Julian. "Pantyhouse." *New Statesman*, 94 (21 Oct. 1977), 556–57. [p. 557]

French, Philip. "Communing with Camus." *The* (London) *Times Literary Supplement*, 28 Oct. 1977, p. 1259.

(unsigned.) *The Washington Post Book World*, 11 Dec. 1977, p. E2.

(unsigned.) "A Christmas Potpourri of Books." *The Wall Street Journal*, 15 Dec. 1977, p. 20.

Cashin, Edward J. "History as Mores: Walker Percy's *Lancelot*." *The Georgia Review*, 31 (Winter 1977), 875–80.

Becker, Tom. *The New Orleans Review*, 5, No. 4 (1978), 363–64.

Daniel, Robert D. "Walker Percy's Lancelot: Secular Raving and Religious Silence." *The Southern Review*, NS 14 (Winter 1978), 186–94.

Epstein, Seymour. *Denver Quarterly*, 12 (Winter 1978), 97–98.

Milton, Edith. "Seven Recent Novels." *The Yale Review*, 67 (Winter 1978), 260–71. [pp. 268–70]

Sullivan, Walter. "The Insane and the Indifferent: Walker Percy and Others." *The Sewanee Review*, 86 (Winter 1978), 153–59. [pp. 157–59]

Lee, Hermione. "Poe Faced." *New Review*, 4 (Dec. 1977-Jan. 1978), 73–74.

Stuttaford, Genevieve. *Publishers' Weekly*, 213 (6 Feb. 1978), 100.

Iyer, Pico. "A Sad Tidiness: Walker Percy and the South." *London Magazine*, NS 18 (Apr. 1978), 62–66.

(unsigned.) *The New York Times Book Review*, 23 Apr. 1978, p. 43.

Smith, Larry. "A Flood of Catholic Novels." *The Critic*, 37 (Dec. 1978), 1–8. [pp. 6–7]

Hobbs, Janet H. In *Masterplots 1978 Annual*. Ed. Frank N. Magill. Englewood Cliffs, NJ: Salem Press, 1978. Pp. 251–53.

S[hoemaker], D[onna]. "Books of Walker Percy." *The Chronicle (of Higher Education) Review*, 5 Mar. 1979, p. R11.

II. CONTRIBUTIONS TO BOOKS AND PERIODICALS

"The Willard Huntington Wright Murder Case." *Carolina Magazine*, 64 (Jan. 1935), 4–6.

"Reviewing the Books" (Rev. of *This Was Ivor Trent*, by Claude Houghton). *Carolina Magazine*, 64 (Feb. 1935), 28.

"The Movie Magazine: A Low 'Slick.'" *Carolina Magazine*, 64 (Mar. 1935), 4–9.

"Reviewing the Books" (Rev. of *Francis the First*, by Francis Hackett). *Carolina Magazine*, 64 (Apr. 1935), 29.

"Symbol as Need." *Thought*, 29 (Autumn 1954), 381–90. [In *MB*, pp. 288–97]

"Symbol as Hermeneutic in Existentialism." *Philosophy and Phenomenological Research*, 16 (June 1956), 522–30. [In *MB*, pp. 277–87]

"Stoicism in the South." *The Commonweal*, 64 (6 July 1956), 342–44.

"The Man on the Train: Three Existential Modes." *Partisan Review*, 23 (Fall 1956), 478–94. [In *MB*, pp. 83–100]

"The Coming Crisis in Psychiatry." *America*, 96 (5 Jan. 1957), 391–93; 96 (12 Jan. 1957), 415–18.

"The American War." *The Commonweal*, 65 (29 Mar. 1957), 655–57.

"Semiotic and a Theory of Knowledge." *The Modern Schoolman*, 34 (May 1957), 225–46. [In *MB*, pp. 243–64]

"Truth—or Pavlov's Dogs?" (Rev. of *Battle for the Mind*, by William Sargant). *America*, 97 (8 June 1957), 306–307.

"The Act of Naming." *Forum* (University of Houston), 1 (Summer 1957), 4–9. [As "The Mystery of Language" in *MB*, pp. 150–58]

"A Southern View." *America*, 97 (20 July 1957), 428–29.

"The Southern Moderate." *The Commonweal*, 67 (13 Dec. 1957), 279–82.

"Metaphor as Mistake." *The Sewanee Review*, 66 (Winter 1958), 79–99. [In *MB*, pp. 64–82]

"Decline of the Western." *The Commonweal*, 68 (16 May 1958), 181–83.

"Symbol, Consciousness, and Intersubjectivity." *The Journal of Philosophy*, 55 (17 July 1958), 631–41. [In *MB*, pp. 265–76]

"The Loss of the Creature." *Forum* (University of Houston), 2 (Fall 1958), 6–14. [In *MB*, pp. 46–63]

"Culture: The Antinomy of the Scientific Method." *The New Scholasticism*, 32 (Oct. 1958), 443–75. [In *MB*, pp. 215–42]

"The Culture Critics." *The Commonweal*, 70 (5 June 1959), 247–50.

"The Message in the Bottle." *Thought*, 34 (Autumn 1959), 405–33. [In *MB*, pp. 119–49]

"Naming and Being." *The Personalist*, 41 (Spring 1960), 148–57.

"Carnival in Gentilly." *Forum* (University of Houston), 3 (Summer 1960), 4–18. [An early version of a portion of *The Moviegoer*]

"The Symbolic Structure of Interpersonal Process." *Psychiatry*, 24 (Feb. 1961), 39–52. [In *MB*, pp. 189–214]

"Modern Man on the Threshold" (Rev. of *Man, God and Magic*, by Ivar Lissner). *America*, 105 (12 Aug. 1961), 612.

"Red, White, and Blue-Gray." *The Commonweal*, 75 (22 Dec. 1961), 337–39.

"Virtues and Vices in the Southern Literary Renascence" (Rev. of *A Dream of Mansions*, by Norris Lloyd; *The Wandering of Desire*, by Marion Montgomery; *Judgment Day*, by Thomas Chastain). *The Commonweal*, 76 (11 May 1962), 181–82.

"How to Succeed in Business without Thinking about Money." *The Commonweal*, 77 (22 Feb. 1963), 557–59.

"Hughes's Solipsism Malgré Lui" (Rev. of *The Fox in the Attic*, by Richard Hughes). *The Sewanee Review*, 72 (Summer 1964), 489–95.

"Mississippi: The Fallen Paradise." *Harper's Magazine*, 230 (Apr. 1965), 166–72.

"The Fire This Time" (Rev. of *"I Do So Politely": A Voice from the South*, by Robert Canzoneri; *Mississippi Black Power*; *Three for Mississippi*, by William Bradford Hule; *Letters from Mississippi*, ed. Elizabeth Sutherland; *Integration at Ole Miss*, by Russell H. Barrett; *Mississippi: The Long Hot Summer*, by William McCord; *Freedom Summer*, by Sally Belfrage). *The New York Review of Books*, 4 (1 July 1965), 3–5.

"The Failure and the Hope." *Katallagete*, 1 (Dec. 1965), 16–21.

"*The Last Gentleman*: Two Excerpts from the Forthcoming Novel." *Harper's Magazine*, 232 (May 1966), 54–56, 59–61.

"From Facts to Fiction." *Book Week*, 4 (25 Dec. 1966), 6, 9.

"The Doctor Listened" (Rev. of *Children of Crisis*, by Robert Coles). *The New York Times Book Review*, 25 June 1967, p. 7.

"Notes for a Novel about The End of the World." *Katallagete*, Winter 1967–68, pp. 7–14. [In *MB*, pp. 101–18]

"New Orleans Mon Amour." *Harper's Magazine*, 237 (Sept. 1968), 80–82, 86, 88, 90.

"Eudora Welty in Jackson." *Shenandoah*, 20 (Spring 1969), 37–38.

Review of *Symbolic Behavior*, by Theodore Thass-Thienemann. *Psychiatry*, 33 (Feb. 1970), 132–34.

"Walter M. Miller, Jr.'s *A Canticle for Leibowitz*." In *Rediscoveries*. Ed. with an intro. by David Madden. New York: Crown, 1971. Pp. 262–69.

"The Mercy Killing." *The New York Times Book Review*, 6 June 1971, p. 7. [Brautigan parody]

Review of *Confessions of a White Racist*, by Larry L. King. *The New York Times Book Review*, 27 June 1971, p. 5.

"Toward a Triadic Theory of Meaning." *Psychiatry*, 35 (Feb. 1972), 1–19. [In *MB*, pp. 159–88]

"Introduction." In *Lanterns on the Levee: Recollections of a Planter's Son*, by William Alexander Percy. Baton Rouge: Louisiana State Univ. Press, 1973. Pp. vii–xviii.

"The Left Hand of Sheed" (Rev. of *People Will Always Be Kind*, by Wilfrid Sheed). *America*, 128 (12 May 1973), 438–39.

" 'Uncle Will' and His South." *Saturday Review/World*, 1 (6 Nov. 1973), 22–25.

"The Delta Factor." *The Southern Review*, NS 11 (Jan. 1975), 29–64. [In *MB*, pp. 3–45]

"A Theory of Language." In *MB*, pp. 298–327.

"Bourbon." *Esquire*, 84 (Dec. 1975), 148–49.

"The State of the Novel: Dying Art or New Science?" *Michigan Quarterly Review*, 16 (Fall 1977), 359–73.

"Random Thoughts on Southern Literature, Southern Politics, and the American Future." *The Georgia Review*, 32 (Fall 1978), 499–511.

Review of Henrik Rosenmeier, ed., *Letters and Documents*, by Søren Kierkegaard. *The New York Times Book Review*, 1 Apr. 1979, pp. 1, 28–29.

III. INTERVIEWS, PANEL DISCUSSIONS, AND OTHER PRINTED REMARKS

"Seven Laymen Discuss Morality." *America*, 104 (1 Oct. 1960), 10–13. [pp. 12–13]

Serebnick, Judith. "First Novelists—Spring 1961." *Library Journal*, 86 (1 Feb. 1961), 597–613. [p. 597]

"Address of Walker Percy, Fiction Winner, National Book Awards, March 13, 1962." [Distributed at the 1962 National Book Awards meeting]

Doar, Harriet. "Walker Percy: He Likes to Put Protagonist in Situation." *The Charlotte* (NC) *Observer*, 30 Sept. 1962, p. D6.

Keith, Don L. "Walker Percy Talks of Many Things." *Delta Review*, 3 (May-June 1966), 38–39.

"Work and Play." *The New York Times Book Review*, 5 June 1966, pp. 1, 60–62. [p. 61]

Brown, Ashley. "An Interview with Walker Percy." *Shenandoah*, 18 (Spring 1967), 3–10.

Franklin, Lynn. "How to Get Ahead: In Fine Arts, In Writing." *The* (New Orleans) *Times-Picayune Dixie Roto Magazine*, 24 Sept. 1967, pp. 11, 46–47. [pp. 46–47]

Cremeens, Carlton. "Walker Percy, The Man and the Novelist: An Interview." *The Southern Review*, NS 4 (Spring 1968), 271–90.

Gallo, Louis. "Walker Percy: Politics, Racism & Literature in the New South." *Vieux Carré Courier* (New Orleans), 13 Nov. 1970, p. 3.

"Comments Made by Walker Percy at the Spring Authors Press Conference on March 3, 1971 in New York during National Book Award Week." [Distributed at the 1971 National Book Awards meeting; excerpt rpt. in *Publishers' Weekly*, 199 (22 Mar. 1971), 23–24]

Carter, Philip D. "Oh, You Know Uncle Walker." *The Washington Post*, 17 June 1971, pp. C1, C4.

Bunting, Charles T. "An Afternoon with Walker Percy." *Notes on Mississippi Writers*, 4 (Fall 1971), 43–61.

Carr, John. "An Interview with Walker Percy." *The Georgia Review*, 25 (Fall 1971), 317–32.

East, Charlie. "Sniper Fiction Comes True." *The* (New Orleans) *Times-Picayune*, 11 Jan. 1973, Sec. 1, pp. 1, 16.

Gallo, Louis. "Walker Percy Struggles with Unbelief." *New Orleans Courier*, 21-27 Sept. 1973, pp. 10–11.

Abádi-Nagy, Zoltán. "A Talk with Walker Percy." *The Southern Literary Journal*, 6 (Fall 1973), 3–19.

Buckley, William F., Jr. "The Southern Imagination: An Interview with Eudora Welty and Walker Percy." *Mississippi Quarterly*, 26 (Fall 1973), 493–516.

King, Barbara. "Walker Percy Prevails." *Southern Voices*, 1 (May-June 1974), 19–23.

Dewey, Bradley R. "Walker Percy Talks about Kierkegaard: An Annotated Interview." *The Journal of Religion*, 54 (July 1974), 273–98.

Mongelluzzo, Bill. "Novelist Bored, Turns to Essays." *The* (New Orleans) *Times-Picayune*, 16 May 1975, Sec. 5, p. 7.

"A Symposium on Fiction: Donald Barthelme, William Gass, Grace Paley, Walker Percy." *Shenandoah*, 27 (Winter 1976), 3–31.

Smith, Marcus. "Talking about Talking: An Interview with Walker Percy." *The New Orleans Review*, 5, No. 1 (1976), 13–18.

Ball, Millie. "Walker Percy Star of Authors' Day." *The* (New Orleans) *Times-Picayune*, 1 Aug. 1976, Sec. 6, p. 18.

Cook, Bruce. "New Faces in Faulkner Country." *Saturday Review*, 3 (4 Sept. 1976), 39–41. [p. 41]

Mitgang, Herbert. "A Talk with Walker Percy." *The New York Times Book Review*, 20 Feb. 1977, pp. 1, 20–21.

Newcombe, Jack. "About Walker Percy." *Book-of-the-Month Club News*, Mar. 1977, p. 4.

Baker, John F. "PW Interviews: Walker Percy." *Publishers' Weekly*, 211 (21 Mar. 1977), 6–7.

Mulligan, Hugh A. "Ills of the Human Condition Diagnosed by Novelist Percy." *The* (New Orleans) *Times-Picayune*, 10 July 1977, Sec. 2, p. 4.

Percy, Walker. "Questions They Never Asked Me." *Esquire*, 88 (Dec. 1977), 170, 172, 184, 186, 188, 190, 193–94.

Mulligan, Hugh A. "Doctor Is In—at the Typewriter." *Los Angeles Times*, 4 Dec. 1977, Part V, pp. 18–19.

Boozer, William. "Percy Fans Have Something to Look Forward to." *The Nashville* (TN) *Banner*, 8 Apr. 1978, p. 5.

"Immortal Nominations." *The New York Times Book Review*, 3 June 1979, pp. 12–13, 51. [p. 51]

IV. BIOGRAPHY AND CRITICISM

[*The Moviegoer*]

Atkins, Anselm. "Walker Percy and Post-Christian Search." *The Centennial Review*, 12 (1968), 73–95.

Bryant, Jerry H. *The Open Decision: The Contemporary American Novel and its Intellectual Background*. New York: Free Press, 1970. [pp. 273-77]

Byrd, Scott. "Mysteries and Movies: Walker Percy's College Articles and *The Moviegoer*." *Mississippi Quarterly*, 25 (1972), 165–81.

Doar, Harriet. "Former UNC Student Wins Novel Award." *The Charlotte* (NC) *Observer*, 14 Mar. 1962, p. B12.

Henisey, Sarah. O. "Intersubjectivity in Symbolization." *Renascence*, 20 (1968), 208–14.

Hobbs, Janet. "Binx Bolling and the Stages on Life's Way." In Broughton, pp. 37–49.

Kazin, Alfred. *Bright Book of Life: American Novelists and Storytellers from Hemingway to Mailer*. Boston: Little, Brown, 1974. [pp. 60–67]

Kostelanetz, Richard. "The New American Fiction." In *The New American Arts*. Ed. Richard Kostelanetz. New York: Horizon Press, 1965. Pp. 194–236. [pp. 224–25]

Lischer, Tracy Kenyon. "Walker Percy's Kierkegaard: A Reading of *The Moviegoer*." *The Cresset*, 41, No. 10 (1978), 10–12.

Luschei, Martin. "*The Moviegoer* as Dissolve." In Broughton, pp. 24–36.

Pindell, Richard. "Basking in the Eye of the Storm: The Esthetics of Loss in Walker Percy's *The Moviegoer*." *boundary 2*, 4 (1975), 219–30.

Presley, Del. "Walker Percy's 'Larroes.' " *Notes on Contemporary Literature*, 3, No. 1 (1973), 5–6.

Quagliano, Anthony. "Existential Modes in *The Moviegoer*." *Research Studies* (Washington State University), 45 (1977), 214–23.

Shepherd, Allen. "Percy's *The Moviegoer* and Robert Penn Warren's *All the King's Men*." *Notes on Mississippi Writers*, 4 (1971), 2–14.

Sims, Barbara B. "Jaybirds as Portents of Hell in Percy and Faulkner." *Notes on Mississippi Writers*, 9 (1976), 24–27.

Sullivan, Walter. "Southerners in the City: Flannery O'Connor and Walker Percy." In *The Comic Imagination in American Literature*. Ed. Louis D. Rubin, Jr. New Brunswick, NJ: Rutgers Univ. Press, 1973. Pp. 339–48.

Thale, Jerome. "Alienation on the American Plan." *Forum* (University of Houston), 6, No. 3 (1968), 36–40.

Thale, Mary. "The Moviegoer in the 1950's." *Twentieth Century Literature*, 14 (1968), 84–89.

(unsigned.) "Story of a Novel: How It Won Prize." *The New York Times*, 15 Mar. 1962, p. 25.

(unsigned.) "The Sustaining Stream." *Time*, 81(1 Feb. 1963), 82–84. [p. 82]

Van Cleave, Jim. "Versions of Percy." *The Southern Review*, NS 6 (1970), 990–1010.

Vauthier, Simone. "Narrative Triangle and Triple Alliance: A Look at *The Moviegoer*." In *Les Américanistes: New French Criticism on Modern American Fiction*. Ed. Ira Johnson and Christiane Johnson. Port Washington, NY: Kennikat, 1978. Pp. 71–93.

———. "Le Temps et la Mort dans *The Movie-Goer*." *Recherches Anglaises et Américaines*, No. 4 (1971), pp. 98–115.

———. "Title as Microtext: The Example of *The Moviegoer*." *The Journal of Narrative Technique*, 5 (1975), 219–29.

Webb, Max. "Binx Bolling's New Orleans: Moviegoing, Southern Writing, and Father Abraham." In Broughton, pp. 1–23.

Weinberg, Helen. *The New Novel in America: The Kafkan Mode in Contemporary Fiction*. Ithaca, NY, and London: Cornell Univ. Press, 1970. [pp. x, xii, 182–83]

[The Last Gentleman]

Broughton, Panthea Reid. "Gentlemen and Fornicators: *The Last Gentleman* and a Bisected Reality." In Broughton, pp. 96–114.

Douglas, Ellen. *Walker Percy's* The Last Gentleman: *Introduction and Commentary*. New York: Seabury Press, 1969.

Hall, Constance. "The Ladies in *The Last Gentleman*." *Notes on Mississippi Writers*, 11, No. 1 (1978), 26–35.

LeClair, Thomas. "Death and Black Humor." *Critique*, 17, No. 1 (1975), 5–40.

Pindell, Richard. "Toward Home: Place, Language, and Death in *The Last Gentleman*." In Broughton, pp. 50–68.

Tanner, Tony. *City of Words: American Fiction 1950–1970*. New York: Harper & Row, 1971. [pp. 260–62]

Tenenbaum, Ruth Betsy. "Walker Percy's 'Consumer-Self' in *The Last Gentleman*." *Louisiana Studies*, 15 (1976), 304–309.

Vauthier, Simone. "Narrative Triangulation in *The Last Gentleman*." In Broughton, pp. 69–95.

Watkins, Floyd C. *The Death of Art: Black and White in the Recent Southern Novel*. Athens: Univ. of Georgia Press, 1970. [pp. 28, 37–38, 47, 58–59]

[*Love in the Ruins*]

Berrigan, J. R. "An Explosion of Utopias." *Moreana*, No. 38 (1973), pp. 21–26.
Cogell, Elizabeth Cummins. "The Middle-Landscape Myth in Science Fiction." *Science-Fiction Studies*, 5 (1978), 134–42. [pp. 138–41]
Godshalk, William Leigh. "*Love in the Ruins*: Thomas More's Distorted Vision." In Broughton, pp. 137–56.
———. "Walker Percy's Christian Vision." *Louisiana Studies*, 13 (1974), 130–41.
Kennedy, J. Gerald. "The Sundered Self and the Riven World: *Love in the Ruins*." In Broughton, pp. 115–36.
LeClair, Thomas. "Walker Percy's Devil." *The Southern Literary Journal*, 10, No. 1 (1977), 3–13. [In Broughton, pp. 157–68]
Sivley, Sherry. "Percy's Down Home Version of More's *Utopia*." *Notes on Contemporary Literature*, 7, No. 4 (1977), 3–5.
Weber, Brom. "The Mode of 'Black Humor.' " In *The Comic Imagination in American Literature*. Ed. Louis D. Rubin, Jr. New Brunswick, NJ: Rutgers Univ. Press, 1973. Pp. 361–71.
Westendorp, T. A. "Recent Southern Fiction: Percy, Price and Dickey." In *Handelingen van het XXIX*e *Vlaams Filologencongres: Antwerpen 16–18 april 1973*. Ed. J. Van Haver. Zellik, Belgium: Vlaamse Filologencongressen, 1973. Pp. 188–98. [pp. 195–98]

[*The Message in the Bottle*]

Poteat, William H. "Reflections on Walker Percy's Theory of Language." In Broughton, pp. 192–218.
Thornton, Weldon. "Homo Loquens, Homo Symbolificus, Homo Sapiens: Walker Percy on Language." In Broughton, pp. 169–91.

[*Lancelot*]

Dowie, William J. "*Lancelot* and the Search for Sin." In Broughton, pp. 245–59.
Kreyling, Michael. "*Crime and Punishment*: The Pattern Beneath the Surface of Percy's *Lancelot*." *Notes on Mississippi Writers*, 11, No. 1 (1978), 36–44.
Lawson, Lewis A. "The Fall of the House of Lamar." In Broughton, pp. 219–44.

[General Studies]

Binding, Paul. *Separate Country: A Literary Journey through the American South*. New York: Paddington Press, 1979. [pp. 33, 69–76, 147, 199, 209, 213; includes printed remarks by Percy]
[Bischoff, Joan]. "Walker Percy." In *American Novelists Since World War II*. Ed. Jeffrey Helterman and Richard Layman. Detroit: Gale, 1978. Pp. 390–97.
Blouin, Michel T. "The Novels of Walker Percy: An Attempt at Synthesis." *Xavier University Studies*, 6 (1967), 29–42.
Bradbury, John M. "Absurd Insurrection: The Barth-Percy Affair." *The South Atlantic Quarterly*, 68 (1969), 319–29.

Bradley, Jared W. "Walker Percy and the Search for Wisdom." *Louisiana Studies*, 12 (1973), 579–90.

*Broberg, Jan. "Walker Percy—En udda amerikan." *Studiekamraten*, 54 (1972), 119–20.

Brooks, Cleanth. "The Current State of American Literature." *The Southern Review*, NS 9 (1973), 273–87. [pp. 285–87]

———. "Walker Percy and Modern Gnosticism." *The Southern Review*, NS 13 (1977), 677–87. [In Broughton, pp. 260–72]

Broughton, Panthea Reid, ed. with an intro. *The Art of Walker Percy: Stratagems for Being*. Baton Rouge: Louisiana State Univ. Press, 1979.

Byrd, Scott. "The Dreams of Walker Percy." *Red Clay Reader*, No. 3 (1966), pp. 70–73.

Chesnick, Eugene. "Novel's Ending and the World's End: The Fiction of Walker Percy." *The Hollins Critic*, 10, No. 5 (1973), 1–11.

Coles, Robert. "Profiles (Walker Percy): The Search." *The New Yorker*, 54 (2 Oct. 1978), 43–44, 47–48, 50, 52, 57–58, 60, 62, 67–68, 70, 72, 74, 79–80, 82, 84, 86, 91–96, 98–106, 109–10; 54 (9 Oct. 1978), 52–54, 57–60, 65–66, 68, 71–72, 74, 77–79, 82, 84, 88, 90, 92, 94, 99–100, 102–104, 106, 109–16, 119–22, 125.

———. *Walker Percy: An American Search*. Boston: Little, Brown, 1979.

Cook, Bruce. "The Search for an American Catholic Novel." *American Libraries*, 4 (1973), 547–49. [p. 549]

Dabbs, James McBride. "Walker Percy." In *Civil Rights in Recent Southern Fiction*. Atlanta, GA: Southern Regional Council, 1969. Pp. 65–73.

Dowie, William. "Walker Percy: Sensualist-Thinker." *Novel*, 6 (1972), 52–65.

Gaston, Paul L. "The Revelation of Walker Percy." *The Colorado Quarterly*, 20 (1972), 459–70.

Hardy, John Edward. "Percy, Walker." In *Encyclopedia of World Literature in the Twentieth Century*. 4 vols. Ed. Frederick Ungar and Lina Mainiero. IV (New York: Ungar, 1975), 278, 281.

Hoffman, Frederick J. *The Art of Southern Fiction: A Study of Some Modern Novelists*. With a preface by Harry T. Moore. Carbondale and Edwardsville: Southern Illinois Univ. Press, 1967. [pp. 129–37]

Johnson, Mark. "The Search for Place in Walker Percy's Novels." *The Southern Literary Journal*, 8, No. 1 (1975), 55–81.

Kazin, Alfred. "The Pilgrimage of Walker Percy." *Harper's Magazine*, 242 (June 1971), 81–86.

Kirby, Jack Temple. *Media-Made Dixie: The South in the American Imagination*. Baton Rouge and London: Louisiana State Univ. Press, 1978. [pp. 160, 164–65]

Kissel, Susan S. "Walker Percy's 'Conversions.'" *The Southern Literary Journal*, 9, No. 2 (1977), 124–36.

Lauder, Robert E. "The Catholic Novel and the 'Insider God.'" *Commonweal*, 101 (25 Oct. 1974), 78–81.

Lawson, Lewis A. "Kierkegaard and the Modern American Novel." In *Essays in Memory of Christine Burleson*. Ed. Thomas G. Burton. Johnson City: East Tennessee State Univ., 1969. Pp. 111–25. [pp. 124–25]

———. "Walker Percy: The Physician as Novelist." *South Atlantic Bulletin*, 37, No. 2 (1972), 58–63.

———. "Walker Percy (1916—)." In *Southern Writers: A Biographical Dictionary*. Ed. Robert Bain, Joseph M. Flora, and Louis D. Rubin, Jr. Baton Rouge and London: Louisiana State Univ. Press, 1979. Pp. 346–47.

———. "Walker Percy's Indirect Communications." *Texas Studies in Literature and Language*, 11 (1969), 867–900.

———. "Walker Percy's Southern Stoic." *The Southern Literary Journal*, 3, No. 1 (1970), 5–31.

LeClair, Thomas. "The Eschatological Vision of Walker Percy." *Renascence*, 26 (1974), 115–22.

Lehan, Richard. *A Dangerous Crossing: French Literary Existentialism and the Modern American Novel*. With a preface by Harry T. Moore. Carbondale and Edwardsville: Southern Illinois Univ. Press, 1973. [pp. 133–45]

———. "The Way Back: Redemption in the Novels of Walker Percy." *The Southern Review*, NS 4 (1968), 306–19.

Luschei, Martin. *The Sovereign Wayfarer: Walker Percy's Diagnosis of the Malaise*. Baton Rouge: Louisiana State Univ. Press, 1972.

Maxwell, Robert. "Walker Percy's Fancy." *The Minnesota Review*, 7 (1967), 231–37.

Murray, Albert. *South to a Very Old Place*. New York: McGraw-Hill, 1971. [pp. 197–209; includes printed remarks by Percy]

Rubin, Louis D., Jr. "The South's Writers: A Literature of Time and Change." *Southern World*, 1, No. 2 (1979), 26–27.

———, et al. "Deep Delta." In *Mississippi Writers in Context: Transcripts of A Climate for Genius, A Television Series*. Ed. Robert L. Phillips, Jr. Jackson, MS: Mississippi Library Commission, 1976. Pp. 17–33. [pp. 21–22, 25–27]

———, et al. "Twentieth-Century Southern Literature." In *Southern Literary Study: Problems and Possibilities*. Ed. Louis D. Rubin, Jr., and C. Hugh Holman. Chapel Hill: Univ. of North Carolina Press, 1975. Pp. 133–64. [pp. 138–41]

Simpson, Lewis P. "The Southern Aesthetic of Memory." *Tulane Studies in English*, 23 (1978), 207–27. [pp. 221–26]

———. "Southern Fiction." In *Harvard Guide to Contemporary American Writing*. Ed. Daniel Hoffman. Cambridge, MA, and London: Belknap Press of Harvard Univ. Press, 1979. Pp. 153–90. [pp. 180–83]

Skelton, Billy. "Percy Novels Satirical Chronicle of Fallen World." Jackson, MS, *Clarion-Ledger*, 15 Mar. 1979, p. B5.

Spivey, Ted R. "Religion and Reintegration of Man in Flannery O'Connor and Walker Percy." *Spectrum* (Georgia State University), 2 (1972), 67–79.

———. "Walker Percy and the Archetypes." In Broughton, pp. 273–93.

Stelzmann, Rainulf A. "Adam in Extremis: Die Romane Walker Percys." *Stimmen der Zeit*, 191 (1973), 206–10.

———. "Das Schwert Christi: Zwei Versuche Walker Percys." *Stimmen der Zeit*, 195 (1977), 641–43.

Stuckey, W. J. "Percy, Walker." In *Contemporary Novelists*. 2nd ed. Ed. James Vinson. New York: St. Martin's Press, 1976. Pp. 1074–75.

Sullivan, Walter. *A Requiem for the Renascence: The State of Fiction in the Modern South*. Athens: Univ. of Georgia Press, 1976. [pp. 64–69, 72–73]

Sullivan, William A., Jr. *Walker Percy*. Jackson, MS: Mississippi Library Commission, 1977.

Tanner, Tony. *The Reign of Wonder: Naivety and Reality in American Literature*. Cambridge, England: Cambridge Univ. Press, 1965. [pp. 349–56]

Taylor, Lewis J., Jr. "Walker Percy and the Self." *Commonweal*, 100 (10 May 1974), 233–36.

———. "Walker Percy's Knights of the Hidden Inwardness." *Anglican Theological Review*, 56 (1974), 125–51.

Telotte, J. P. "Walker Percy's Language of Creation." *The Southern Quarterly*, 16 (1978), 105–16.

Torrens, James. "Walker Percy's Bicentennial Message." *America*, 133 (25 Oct. 1975), 256–58.

(unsigned.) "Loyola to Give Honor Degrees." *The* (New Orleans) *Times-Picayune*, 14 May 1972, Sec. 1, p. 12.

(unsigned.) "North Lee Road: Something Old and Something New in Covington." *The* (New Orleans) *Times-Picayune*, 24 July 1977, Sec. 4, pp. 1–2.

(unsigned.) "Percy, Walker." *Current Biography*, 37 (Sept. 1976), 14–17.

(unsigned.) "Percy, Walker." In *World Authors, 1950–1970*. Ed. John Wakeman. New York: Wilson, 1975. Pp. 1126–28.

Zeugner, John F. "Walker Percy and Gabriel Marcel: The Castaway and the Wayfarer." *Mississippi Quarterly*, 28 (1974–75), 21–53.

[Dissertations and Theses]

Alterman, Peter Steven. "A Study of Four Science Fiction Themes and Their Function in Two Contemporary Novels." Diss. University of Denver, 1974. [*DAI*, 35: 2976A-77A]

Atkins, George Tyng Anselm, Jr. "Freedom, Fate, Myth, and Other Theological Issues in Some Contemporary Literature." Diss. Emory University, 1971. [*DAI*, 32: 6529A]

Auer, Michael Joseph. "Angels and Beasts: Gnosticism in American Literature." Diss. University of North Carolina at Chapel Hill, 1976. [*DAI*, 37: 5117A]

Barnwell, Marion G. "Walker Percy's American Trilogy." Thesis, Mississippi State University, 1974.

Bates, Marvin Randolph. "Walker Percy's Ironic Apology." Diss. Tulane University, 1978. [*DAI*, 39: 6755A]

Bergen, Daniel Patrick. "In Fear of Abstraction: The Southern Response to the North in Twentieth-Century Fiction and Non-Fiction." Diss. University of Minnesota, 1970. [*DAI*, 31: 5389A]

Bischoff, Joan. "With Manic Laughter: The Secular Apocalypse in American Novels of the 1960's." Diss. Lehigh University, 1975. [*DAI*, 36: 2818A]

Borgman, Paul. "The Symbolic City and Christian Existentialism in Fiction by Flannery O'Connor, Walker Percy, and John Updike." Diss. University of Chicago, 1973.

Cass, Michael McConnell. "Stages on the South's Way: Walker Percy's *The Moviegoer* and *The Last Gentleman*." Diss. Emory University, 1971. [*DAI*, 32: 3992A]

Davies, Douglas D. "The Possibilities of the Hero in Three Contemporary Novels." Thesis, San Francisco State College, 1966.

Doran, Linda Kay Dyer. "Naming as Disclosure: A Study of Theme and Method in the Fiction of Walker Percy." Diss. George Peabody College for Teachers, 1976. [*DAI*, 37: 2179A]

Foley, I. M. "The Theory of Language in Walker Percy's *The Message in the Bottle*." Thesis, University of New Orleans, 1975.

Foster, M. "Pain and Death in James Dickey's *Deliverance* and the Novels of Walker Percy." Thesis, University of Houston, 1975.

Fox, William Henry. "Opposition to Secular Humanism in the Fiction of Flannery O'Connor and Walker Percy." Diss. Emory University, 1979. [*DAI*, 40: 236A-37A]

Freisinger, Randall Roy. " 'To Move Wild Laughter in the Throat of Death': An Anatomy of Black Humor." Diss. University of Missouri-Columbia, 1975. [*DAI*, 36: 6655A]

Gallo, Louis Jacob. "From Malaisian to Saint: A Study of Walker Percy." Diss. University of Missouri-Columbia, 1973. [*DAI*, 34: 7230A-31A]

Gray, Richardson K. "A Christian-Existentialist: The Vision of Walker Percy." Diss. Ohio University, 1978. [*DAI*, 39: 6761A]

Hall, Constance H. "Walker Percy's Women: A Study of the Women in the Novels of Walker Percy." Thesis, Stephen F. Austin State University, 1975.

Hammond, John Francis. "The Monomythic Quest: Visions of Heroism in Malamud, Bellow, Barth, and Percy." Diss. Lehigh University, 1979. [*DAI*, 39: 6130A]

Haydel, Douglas Joseph. "From the Realistic to the Fantastic: Walker Percy's Expanding Vision." Diss. Florida State University, 1978. [*DAI*, 39: 6762A]

Hicks, Walter Jackson. "An Essay on Recent American Fiction." Diss. University of North Carolina at Chapel Hill, 1974. [*DAI*, 35: 3744A]

Hobbs, Janet H. "Alternatives to Alienation in the Novels of Walker Percy." Thesis, Virginia Polytechnic Institute, 1974.

Jones, Elinor B. "The Search as Pilgrimage in the Novels of Walker Percy." Thesis, University of Georgia, 1975.

Kent, Margaret L. "The Novels of Walker Percy." Thesis, University of North Carolina at Chapel Hill, 1969.

Killough, Barbara C. "*The Moviegoer*: The Search for an Access to Being." Thesis, University of Houston, 1971.

Kissel, Susan Stevens. "For a 'Hostile Audience': A Study of the Fiction of Flannery O'Connor, Walker Percy, and J. F. Powers." Diss. University of Cincinnati, 1975. [*DAI*, 36: 2824A]

LeClair, Thomas Edmund. "Final Words: Death and Comedy in the Fiction of Donleavy, Hawkes, Barth, Vonnegut, and Percy." Diss. Duke University, 1972. [*DAI*, 33: 5731A]

Luschei, Martin Louis. "The Sovereign Wayfarer: Walker Percy's Diagnosis of the Malaise." Diss. University of New Mexico, 1970. [*DAI*, 31: 5414A]

Mack, James Robert. "Love and Marriage in Walker Percy's Novels." Diss. Emory University, 1976. [*DAI*, 37: 4355A-56A]

Madathiparampil, George J. "Theory and Themes in the Novels of Walker Percy." Thesis, Indiana State University, 1978.

Martin, Lovick R. "The Theme of Reconciliation and the Novels of Walker Percy." Diss. University of North Carolina at Chapel Hill, 1972.

Osinski, Barbara H. "From Malaise to Communion: A Study of Walker Percy's *The Moviegoer*." Thesis, Lehigh University, 1972.

Pearson, Michael Patrick. "The Rhetoric of Symbolic Action: Walker Percy's Way of Knowing." Diss. Pennsylvania State University, 1977. [*DAI*, 39: 875A]

Riehl, Robert Ellison. "The Ordeal of Meaning: Walker Percy's Philosophy of Language and His Novels." Diss. University of Texas at Austin, 1975. [*DAI*, 35: 2812A-13A]

Ryan, Steven Tom. "Chaotic Slumber: Picaresque and Gothic in Contemporary American Novels." Diss. University of Utah, 1976. [*DAI*, 37: 2187A]

Sturdivant, Mary E. "Christianity in the Novels of Walker Percy." Diss. University of North Carolina at Chapel Hill, 1972.

Swick, Marly A. "Romantic Ministers and Phallic Knights: A Study of *A Month of Sundays, Lancelot,* and *Falconer*." Diss. The American University, 1979. [*DAI*, 40: 860A]

Taylor, Lewis Jerome, Jr. "The Becoming of Self in the Writings of Walker Percy: A Kierkegaardian Analysis." Diss. Duke University, 1972. [*DAI*, 33: 1224A]

Telotte, Jay Paul. "To Talk Creatively: A Study of the Writings of Walker Percy." Diss. University of Florida, 1976. [*DAI*, 37: 6489A-90A]

Watkins, Suzanne Blackmon. "From Physician to Novelist: The Progression of Walker Percy." Diss. New York University, 1977. [*DAI*, 38: 6196A]

Williams, Mina Gwen. "The Sense of Place in Southern Fiction." Diss. Louisiana State University, 1973. [*DAI*, 34: 3440A-41A]

Wineapple, Brenda. "Neo-Romanticism in Contemporary American Fiction." Diss. University of Wisconsin-Madison, 1976. [*DAI*, 37: 5133A]

Wyche, Charlyne S. "A Survey of the Southern Legend in the Recent Southern Novel." Thesis, McNeese State University, 1969.

Notes on Contributors

RANDOLPH BATES, an instructor in English at Louisiana State University, has published poetry, fiction, and reviews in a number of journals, including *Seattle Review, Cimarron Review, Poetry Now, Bellingham Review* and *INTRO 10*.

CHARLES P. BIGGER is professor of philosophy at Louisiana State University.

ROBERT H. BRINKMEYER, JR., an assistant professor of English at North Carolina Central University, writes regularly for *Southern Exposure*. He is currently at work on a study of Catholic writers of the modern South.

JEROME C. CHRISTENSEN, an assistant professor of English at Purdue University, teaches British Romantic literature and film. He has published several articles on Coleridge and has recently finished a book length manuscript titled *Coleridge and the Blessed Machine of Language*.

CORINNE DALE, an assistant professor at Texas A & M University, teaches American literature and a course in modern Southern fiction. She has published several articles on Southern fiction.

CECIL L. EUBANKS, an associate professor of political science at Louisiana State University, teaches contemporary political theory. His most recent publications include "Reinhold Niebuhr: The Dialectics of Grace and Power" in *The Political Science Reviewer*.

DANIEL H. GANN is First Assistant in the Department of Literature, Philosophy and Religion at the Memphis Public Library, Memphis, Tennessee.

JOHN EDWARD HARDY, professor of English at the University of Illinois at Chicago Circle, is the author of numerous works, including *Katherine Anne Porter* and *Man in the Modern Novel*.

SUSAN S. KISSEL, assistant professor of English at Northern Kentucky University, has published articles on Walker Percy, Robert · Coover, and J. F. Powers.

LEWIS A. LAWSON, a professor of English at the University of Maryland, has long had an interest in Walker Percy's work. His most recent articles on Percy have appeared in *The Stoic Strain in American Literature* and *Stratagems for Being*.

MICHAEL PEARSON, a freelance writer, teaches writing and literature in Hinesburg, Vermont. He has published a number of reviews and has just completed an article on Malamud's *The Natural*.

J. P. TELOTTE, an assistant professor of English at Georgia Institute of Technology, has published a number of essays on Walker Percy and on film.

JOE WEIXLMANN is associate professor of English at Indiana State University and editor of *Black American Literature Forum*. In addition to compiling numerous article-length bibliographies of contemporary American fictionalists, he has authored *John Barth: A Descriptive Primary and Annotated Secondary Bibliography*.